Beyond the Whales

As the sun dips below the horizon many species of fish rise toward the surface, bringing the wealth of the depths within reach of surface dwellers including orca, birds and humans.

Beyond the Whales

The Photographs and Passions of Alexandra Morton

Alexandra Morton

TouchWood Editions

Copyright © 2004 by Alexandra Morton
Photographs, drawings and map © by Alexandra Morton
First edition

Cover photos: Alexandra Morton. Cover and book design: Nancy St.Gelais
This book is set in Adobe Garamond Pro
Printed in Canada

TouchWood Editions Ltd.
Victoria, BC, Canada
www.touchwoodeditions.com
This book is distributed by Heritage House,
#108-17665 66A Avenue, Surrey, BC, Canada, V3S 2A7.

TouchWood Editions acknowledges the financial support for its publishing program from The Canada Council for the Arts, the Government of Canada through the Book Publishing Industry Development Program (BPIDP) and the Province of British Columbia through the British Columbia Arts Council.
National Library of Canada in Cataloguing

Library and Archives Canada Cataloguing in Publication
Morton, Alexandra, 1957-
    Beyond the whales: the photographs and passions of Alexandra Morton/AlexandraMorton.

ISBN 1-894898-23-0

    1. Marine animals—British Columbia—Pacific Coast—Pictorial works. 2. Marine animals—British Columbia—Pacific Coast. 3. Marine ecology—British Columbia—Pacific Coast. 4. Morton, Alexandra, 1957- I.Title.

QL221.B7M67   2004 577.7'433   C2004-905025-7

The Canada Council | Le Conseil des Arts
for the Arts | du Canada

BRITISH
COLUMBIA
ARTS COUNCIL
We acknowledge the support of the Province of British Columbia
through the British Columbia Arts Council

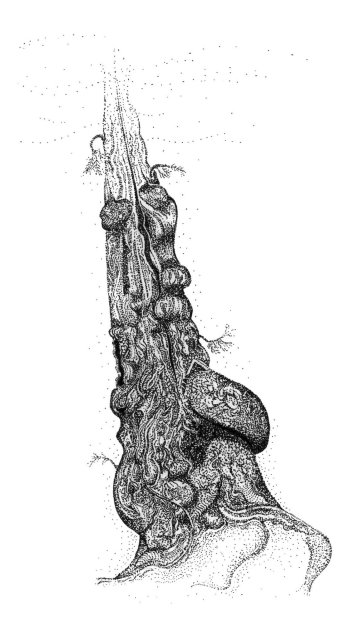

Contents

Acknowledgments

The photographs in this book have lived with me in the Broughton Archipelago, some for over 20 years. The permeating wet and the many moves, from boat to floathouse to land, have damaged some and for that I apologize. We have included these, however, as they capture fleeting images which need to be recorded. Please accept the blemishes as part of the organic nature of art.

Parts of this text have appeared, in different forms, in *WaveLength Paddling Magazine*, in which I write a column. I would like to thank Alan Wilson, the editor, for his consent to use these sections and for his support. I would like to thank Marlyn Horsdal for putting this book together. The salmon-farming issue is so urgent and demanding that this book would certainly not exist without Marlyn. And I would like to thank the Broughton Archipelago for having me and allowing me to raise my children amongst her generosity and safe harbours.

Dedication

This book is dedicated to my children, Jarret and Clio, who will inherit whatever world we create.

*Two orca flow out of Weyton Pass
at sunset on a full-moon ebb tide.*

Foreword

The sun's sparkles bounced from the waters of Fulford Harbour to the dappled shade of our grape arbour. We were having lunch, a lunch I will never forget. The feast my wife Birgit put before us was delightful but it was the company around the picnic table that made the day so memorable. One guest was Jane Goodall, the other Alexandra Morton. We learned that Jane had been Alex's role model from girlhood. This was the first meeting of these brilliant and important women. Jane Goodall has had international stature as a primatologist and educator for many decades. The stature of Alexandra Morton continues to grow.

This is the reason why the arrival of Alex's book, *Beyond the Whales,* is so welcome. Thousands of us have heard her words on radio and television, putting forth the case for a sensible treatment for all forms of life on the coast. Now we have her words and images in print. This book gives a picture of a talented, dedicated and passionate woman and her world. Of the many elegant books on the richness and beauty of the west coast, I know of none better at capturing its treasures. This is done through Alex's eloquent words and her own excellent photos and drawings. She and her family have lived for over two decades an almost saint-like life, Spartan and often risky, in order to be immersed in the world of the orca.

Alexandra Morton brings to us the joy and complexity of that world. Starting with her whales at the top of the food chain, she moves us through the interconnected organisms with strong emphasis on forests and salmon. The Goodall-Morton parallel becomes obvious when we think of chimpanzees and orca as highly evolved, intelligent, social animals. They are remarkable communicators and share with humans a sense of family and kinship. Their plight should touch the hearts of every human being. They are flagships: If these animals can promote the protection of tropical forest or coastal ecosystem, they will have helped not only their own future but that of countless other lifeforms, including humans.

I enjoyed all of the chapters in this book but my favourite is "Fragile Splendour," which lays out the details of the impacts of industrial approaches to logging and fish-farming. I was pleased to read Alex's accolades to the lowly pink salmon. Birgit and I try to eat well-caught pinks twice a week, partly because it is the healthiest of the salmon and partly because doing so supports smaller, local fishing communities. (It tastes great, too.)

Millions of years of evolution have brought this coastal ecosystem to wild perfection. To know it is to love it and to love it is to fight for it. Alexandra Morton's *Beyond the Whales* helps us to know, love and fight. It is worth it on all counts.

Robert Bateman
Salt Spring Island, B.C.

Introduction

When I was 18 I naively thought that if I looked hard enough, I could understand the communication between two whales in a tank in Los Angeles. I was wrong. Those whales were a fragment stolen away from a much larger world; there was no hint of who they really were. So I relocated myself into their environment and tried once again to find the relationship between what the whales were saying and what they were doing.

In the fishbowl setting of an aquarium I could see the whales night and day from above and below, but now the whales became distant plumes of warmed breath, fleeting fins slipping into dark waters and distant voices in the tumult of tidal torrents and tumbling pebbles. To study wild whales one must become a tracker and pay attention to the most subtle clues. Everything must be factored in: the strength of a full-moon spring tide, the sheen of bubbles marking a rising mass of herring, the scent of 5 million pink salmon carried on the breeze. The orca is its environment and so are we.

All biologists who go into the natural world to study an organism become fingertips, conveying messages back to the central nervous system of humanity. My 21 years in an exquisite little archipelago on the west coast of Canada have made it clear to me that this world is one organism. The tides rise and fall the same as my chest when I breathe. The salmon are the bloodstream, moving nutrients between the open ocean and mountain forests. The whales are neighbours trying to make a living. In this book I offer glimpses of how this coastal world works and how it is interconnected. I have collected intimate images that include our species within the array of life.

There is no us and them. "The environment" does not end at the outermost layer of our skin. From the storm clouds of a rising southeasterly storm to the very DNA within each human cell, the environment is a continuum. When some people suggest that we can have jobs or the environment, they are asking you to choose between having cash or your lungs; they are suggesting you give up an essential part of your living self.

Homo sapiens is a clever creature without a doubt. Our ability to imagine something new, something that we have never seen, and then create it is very impressive and wondrous. But we have never existed in a finite world. Our discontent, our explorers and frontiersmen have always had new territory to expand into, until now. With single-minded vision we changed the world to fit us. But these changes were helter-skelter, without design, often based on personal greed, not made with consideration for our species. Now we face a challenge, because our bodies are part of this world we have rearranged. While we might find a way to survive on a degraded planet, is that what we want?

There is great consensus among scientists today that humanity has reached a crossroads. We also concur that we cannot delay our choice of routes because this turning point is alive and coming closer. We cannot retreat because evolution does not allow this. We must use our spectacular brains to figure out which way we are going to go.

We already know the natural laws and systems that work well on Earth because the inheritance bestowed upon us was vast and we have thrived. But like a child with a new hammer, we have delighted in disassembly. In the last hundred years we have explored the concept of: *If we do this, what will happen?* Well, whether we admit it or not, lots *is* now happening as a consequence, and many suspect we are doomed at a cellular level if we stay this course.

My 21 years' examining a spectacular living system have infused me with this question: *What if we tried working with the natural laws instead of against them? What if we looked at a natural system and thought, "How do we fit in here?" instead of looking at it and thinking, "Let's break it; we can always try to fix it later."* Salmon hatcheries fit this paradigm. "Let's take away what salmon need to spawn, because we can always reinvent a salmon that can survive here." This hasn't worked. Pesticides fit this paradigm. "Let's make all life uniform and susceptible to the same disease, then try to get rid of the disease." Hmmm — this definitely hasn't worked. Antibiotics in animal food are part of this experiment. "Let's overcrowd animals and then try to keep them alive." This is starting to kill us.

Our childish ways have released a Pandora's box of woes. The "little guys," as I call the bacteria, viruses and parasites, are having a heyday as a result of our reckless behaviour. *They* are not going extinct; they are flourishing, and they have no qualms about biting the hands that released them!

Here in the Broughton we can harm only a few more cycles of salmon before they are lost to us; we have only a few more years to choose between life and death. The salmon farms must decrease, to bring the little guys under control and allow the wild salmon bloodstream to flow. Worldwide we may have a little more time than that.

I hope this book will communicate some of the perfection of nature and the wisdom of its laws and dynamics that we *do* fit prosperously within. I think we can grow up and mature into a life form capable of surviving. I think we can live in a place without making a mess of it. Parks have been a good idea, but do we really have to build a fence around everything alive and keep ourselves out for it to survive?

The natural world is us; there really is no fence.

Alexandra Morton
Echo Bay

Too often, we humans forget we are positioned precariously at the top of the complex food chain. No matter how technologically able we become, we still need the natural systems which have developed to maintain life on Earth.

Arrival

J came into the wild and lovely Broughton Archipelago with my late husband, the photographer and filmmaker Robin Morton, in 1984, following whales. I am a whale researcher, and all I had eyes for were the orca (formerly called "killer whales") and the magnificent scenery.

❧

Coming into the Archipelago

On a day in the fall of 1984, we were tracking whales from our Zodiac. As we moved farther east, the channel opened into a huge, amphitheatre-like space. Ringed by snow-frosted mountains, the circular body of water was stone silent. There were no distant tugs, cruise ships or fishboat engines roaring underwater. The whales' calls echoed five and six times in the stillness, and we felt we'd been led to the end of the world. As I scanned the expanse through binoculars, I was startled to find a wisp of smoke and beneath it a tiny house floating on the water. The persistent rain had trickled down inside our suits, chilling us through, and we wanted to get Jarret,

Glacier Bay in Knight Inlet speaks of the power and majesty of the inlets. Locked in this glacier field is ancient ice, free of human contaminants, meted out slowly to fuel the dynamic of the tidal inlets' influence on coastal seas.

our two-year-old son, out of the boat. We had considered camping, but the smoke looked more inviting than a wet piece of forest floor, so we left the whales. As we approached the house, we could see that it sat in a small bay with other floating houses. There was a broad white beach at the head of the bay. The chart identified this place as Echo Bay.

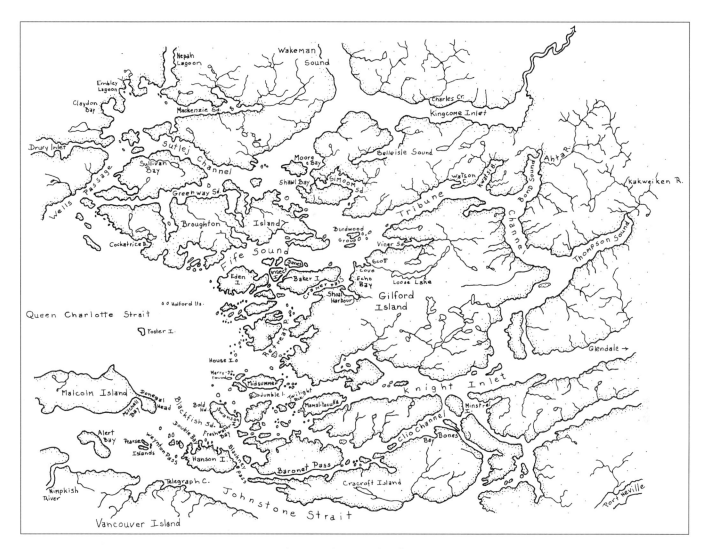

The Broughton Archipelago. It is a living system, providing the essentials for life: clean air, water and food. Systems such as this are required for human life too.

Top: Yakat's family prepares to sleep in Tribune Channel. They form a line all abreast and their breathing becomes very regular. The blows in this image illustrate the orca's ability and preference to breathe in exact unison with friends and family. Whales keep travelling in their sleep, so they would sleep their way around Gilford Island and awake when they reached Knight Inlet.

Bottom left: A male orca "spyhops," raising his keen eyes above the water to look around. Orca have very good vision – as good as a cat's – though their primary sense is sound. The youngsters will peer back at the humans and dogs in boats looking at them.

Bottom right: Pointer (A39 in research nomenclature) streaks south into Blackfish Sound from the White Cliff Islets, heading for good summer fishing and the exuberant rough play between males of the northern resident population.

Orca

The more time we spent on research and photography in the area, the more we came to recognize individual orca and learn something of the meaning of their actions and behaviour.

❧

Whale Culture and Society

When a young Englishwoman named Jane Goodall went into the jungle to study chimpanzees, she was discouraged from naming them. In her doctoral thesis she was told she could not even identify them as "he" or "she"; she had to write "it." But she refused. Today the concept of culture among animals is gaining credibility. We have taken a big step in 30 years.

One of humanity's most successful strategies is that we share realities with each other. Our children do it naturally in their play: "You be the king, I'll be the princess and you are my horse." This ability to agree on who is what and what belongs where has given rise to our diverse cultures. We learn to handle our environment, build cities, create art, practise

Tsitika's son, Pointer, who carries the indisputable sign of his lineage in his unusually curved dorsal fin. He is just entering Blackfish Sound to hunt chinook salmon at "the wall," a famous fishing hole.

An orca splashes its flukes. Summer is a time for play, when abundant salmon allow the whales to gather, and a time for the youngsters to be socialized in the distinct culture of the northern resident orca.

traditions and design governments, until each in turn erodes and we start over again, carrying always a few strands from the previous culture to become our myths.

Now many researchers think something like this may occur among some animal groups. Only certain groups of primates use sticks to fish for termites, wash sand from rice or medicate themselves with plants. The orca also have a culture. When a whale is born into a pod, he or she learns a dialect. If she is a member of the northern resident community, which includes three clans — A, G and R — she will learn where the rubbing beaches are; if she was a daughter of the whale known as Eve, she would have learned where the oolichan-fed chinook rest between tides in Kingcome Inlet.

The range of the three A-clan pods extends from just south of Campbell River, where some were caught years ago in Pender Harbour, north to the Prince Rupert area. They have never been seen in the Queen Charlotte Islands, but they do venture out to the west coast of Vancouver Island and into the open Pacific. While each community of orca — the northern residents, southern residents and transients

Sometimes whales appear to argue about which route to travel. Here Yakat (A11) leads her family into Tribune Channel while her sister, Kelsey (A24), follows, slapping the water with her tail at every surfacing. It is often hard to assign motivation to whale behaviour, so while I see this as an argument, another whale researcher might guess that Kelsey is dislodging an annoying parasite from the underside of her flukes.

— has a home range, these ranges overlap. In the case of the transients, the range is so large we don't even have a clear idea of its dimensions. Johnstone Strait, however, is a very important part of the northern residents' domain, and this community of whales uses the strait in a precise and fascinating way.

Most of the northern community visits Johnstone Strait at least once a summer, and in the 1980s there was one pod that operated an "escort service" into and out of the strait. Nicola's family, with her daughter Tsitika, three grandsons and a tiny granddaughter, were generally the first northern resident whales to enter Johnstone Strait for the summer. They spent a few days feeding on the early runs of chinook salmon and then vanished. Within days they would reappear with another northern resident family.

Whenever Nicola left Johnstone Strait I felt a sense of anticipation — who would she bring back with her this time? Generally, the first arrivals were her close relatives, the other A pods. This group of families shares most calls. We tried to follow Nicola whenever she headed north, and on a few occasions we were lucky enough to watch her greet incoming whales.

The family generally moved fast on greeting duty. The males were the most obviously excited, and they generally overtook their grandmother, rushing ahead in a spectacular swimming mode called "porpoising." A porpoising whale

The lovely Yakat plies the tranquil waters of Tribune Channel. The white finger on the leading edge of her saddle is an identifying mark, along with the little notches at the base of her dorsal fin.

brings its entire body out of the water to breathe in an explosion of glistening whale and spray. When we saw this type of excited behaviour, we learned to drop the hydrophone, listen and scan the horizon. In a short time we could usually spot distant dorsal fins, thin slivers of black, rising and falling to the rhythm of a swimming orca. Many objects mimic an orca's dorsal fin on the horizon: old floating tree roots, sailboats, kayakers or the most deceptive — black pelagic cormorants bobbing gently on a log. As a rule, if you have time to pull out the binoculars and get a good look, it's not an orca.

An orca streaks in hot pursuit of a large chinook salmon during the summer gathering in Johnstone Strait.

When Nicola's family got within a mile or so of the newcomers, they often stopped and let the others approach. These reunions of families made it clear just how social orca are. They were not casual about it — they were intense. The whales mingled in a tangle of fins and sleek black backs. They were in physical contact, pushing and sliding along one another. It was surprising to see how many whales could pile up in a small piece of ocean.

Some meetings were brief, others as long as half an hour, and then the whales would turn and head toward Johnstone Strait together. Once they were travelling, they broke up into smaller groups. Mothers with young calves could be seen side by side, their youngsters frolicking close by. The youngsters popped up and down, chasing, splashing and rolling. Their play was punctuated by brief contact with mum, probably to nurse.

Whale Relationships

A graduate student, Lance Barrett-Lennard studied the genetics of local orca for his doctoral thesis at the University of British Columbia. He took a tiny sample of blubber from as many wild whales as possible and examined their DNA in hopes of determining who the fathers were. No one knew if the whales were mating within their pod or their community. Based on the sounds they make, the community of northern resident whales appears to be divided into the distinct clans of A, G and R, each of which sounds very different from the others. Every pod within these three clans has its own unique derivative of the clan dialect, but all G-clan whales sound similar, as do the A- and R-clan whales. Conversely, As sound very different from Rs or Gs. What Barrett-Lennard discovered is that resident whales generally mate outside their clan, but within their community. Partners

The mighty and handsome Top Notch (A5) hurries south with relatives to join in the summer festivities of their clan, to feast on the abundant runs of salmon in Johnstone Strait.

would therefore have met at the summer gatherings in Johnstone Strait and elsewhere, but whale protocol favours coupling between whales with different dialects. Perhaps it helps prevent this matriarchal society from inbreeding: "If he speaks your dialect — don't mate with him." Barrett-Lennard's research also determined that generally, the males don't start becoming fathers until they are in their late 20s and that many males never become fathers at all.

Talking to a Whale

As I became increasingly familiar with the dialect of the A-clan whales, the "Pituuuu" call that they made fascinated me, particularly its role in facilitating synchrony. One afternoon as we drifted in the open waters of Queen Charlotte Strait, I made the call with my voice to a whale passing close to the boat. It was the large male Top Notch, and his response thrilled me. He dove and reappeared right beside the boat seconds later, his enormous head rising seven or eight feet out of the water. He seemed to be having a look at exactly who, or what, was in the boat.

I don't know what I said to him, but I had the impression I had said something he understood. However, in typical orca fashion, my "speaking" to them never elicited such a response again. I imagined them thinking, "Yeah, yeah, we know you can do that. Show us something new."

Disappearance

I have been studying whales for 20 years, and I've learned not to take them for granted. Each sighting is precious, and I make certain my movements around them are careful and respectful of their needs, because I have witnessed the disappearance of whales.

For the first 10 years I was here, the whales led me on a continuing voyage of discovery. I watched as the families broke down into their smallest divisible units every winter to forage in the kelp beds and winter chinook habitat. I watched the transients — mammal-eaters — a completely different society of whales. I learned these waters "belonged" to the A-clan resident whales, and they fished it with the same precision and success as the best human fishermen of my community. In the spring they arrived to meet the chinook salmon coming down from the heads of the inlets after feeding on oolichan. Then they returned in midsummer to fish the pinks that poured through here on their way to the rivers — the Kakweikan, Ahta, Glendale and Klinaklini. In the fall, they returned with members of G clan to feed on the Viner River chum salmon. I saw birth and death and lived my life on the whales' schedule, always ready to join them — and then they left.

When salmon farms began playing 198-decibel sounds (the level of a jet engine at take-off) underwater in 1993, no

Two male orca at play. Behaviourists note that the larger the brain of a creature, the greater the intelligence, the longer the childhood stage and the more it plays throughout life. Play also tells us that orca do not need to spend every waking minute feeding their large bodies.

Saddle (A14) and her daughter, Sharky (A25), cross Queen Charlotte Strait. Saddle was held captive for some years in Pender Harbour and trained to perform. After her release she gave birth to Sharky, a very outgoing whale who starred in most of Robin's films. Both of these whales have died, but Sharky's daughter is the female who mothered Springer, the lone little whale who was transported north from Puget Sound in 2002.

A high-speed whale glides along the water's surface, moving faster in the air than she can in the water. This is called "porpoising." Orca swim in their sleep, swim during play and swim in pursuit of food. Generally, they move slowly, with great majesty and grace, so to see them swim quickly is a spectacle of enormous power.

one knew what impact this would have, what a deep ripple of disruption would result. Acoustic harassment devices (AHDs), dubbed "acoustic brooms," were considered a benign way of ridding the farms of unwanted attention by hungry seals, better than shooting them. But whales depend on their hearing, and I learned they will not risk it, even if they have to abandon prime fishing territory. One by one the families encountered the noise and turned away, never to return, as if a door had been slammed in their faces. This was a tragedy for me, but it was much worse for the whales, who had to learn to find their food in new places, far from their age-old fishing grounds.

The noise continued for five years and then was turned off, but in that time many whales died. Three of the oldest matriarchs of the A clan — Nicola, Eve and Stripe — died, and with them passed the knowledge of how to fish the chinook of Kingcome. It is easy to take even the magnificent orca for granted, but when they leave, there is no guarantee they will ever return. Hindsight is clear, but it is no way to steer a course.

Hardy (A20) putting on a spectacular display, hanging upside down, waving his tail flukes. This was during the first spring meeting between two families that had spent the winter travelling separately.

Food Resources

I often went fishing with my neighbours, until I learned how to solo, and quickly learned the "hotspots." The best fishermen drop their gear only at precise locations and at exact phases of the tide. If they didn't get a bite, we pulled up the gear and tried another spot. When I followed the whales I quickly noticed they fished exactly the same locations as the humans. They too zigzagged up Kingcome Inlet, not bothering with the vast swaths of coastline in between. Perhaps the knowledge held by the human fishermen came from seeing Eve's ancestors tearing up the water, a huge silver fish glinting ahead. Eve had learned the spots from her mother, and her mother had learned from her mother back a thousand years. Two thousand years?

Brothers Top Notch and Foster (A26) pursuing salmon in Queen Charlotte Strait. Although the chinook salmon are the orca's favourite food, here they are hunting sockeye in the open waters.

Tsitika and her sons, sleeping their way east along the north shore of Malcolm Island.

Every group of orca studied worldwide has habits peculiar to them alone. We think a great deal of this specialization stems from what food resources are available to them. One of the most remarkable glimpses into orca society is the existence of two groups of orca, side by side in B.C. waters, with two distinct cultures.

The transients or mammal-eaters, are quiet. Their dialect is very different from the fish-eaters and they have small families that splinter when they reach the number five. They are nomadic and highly adaptable; if one route becomes blocked, they just figure out another course.

The residents or fish-eaters have big, noisy families. They have a gradient of dialects: close lineages have many shared sounds, and distant lineages are marked by a lack of shared calls. They are very set on routing, insisting on either following the path of the salmon or abandoning the entire area. They have no interest in the back door, and if they are displaced from their traditional winter grounds, I don't know where they go.

These differences can be traced to food. If the transients were chatty, their clever seal and porpoise prey would quietly sneak out of the way when they heard the whales coming. Recent research demonstrated that B.C. seals know the difference between the calls of the fish-eaters and those of the mammal-eaters. Just for insurance, these seals also clump all unknown orca calls, such as Alaskan calls, into the "dangerous" category. A seal, while fat and juicy, is small compared to a school of salmon, so one seal will only feed one or two whales. Many times I have seen the big transient males waiting patiently, eating nothing, while mum and the youngest kid feed on one seal. If there were 20 in the family, it would be a very long time between bites.

Brain and Memory

I always thought whale blows would form dense white clouds, like our breath in winter, but they don't. Whale blows are harder to spot in winter, and snowy hillsides can camouflage what blows they do create. I suspect orca have a way of keeping their breath cool. They are a warm mammal in a cold sea and have many superb design features to allow them this lifestyle. One of the greatest rewards to the whale for staying in the sea is the growth of a large brain, unfettered by gravity and problematic pelvic bones.

The intriguing case of a large brain in a cold ocean is a mystery. Brains are oxygen hungry; no animal that makes a

The scratches on this whale's saddle are teeth marks, the sign of a rowdy bout of play. Male orca, such as this one, play with such excitement that they often rake their teeth over each other's bodies.

Siwiti (A48) slides playfully over the back of her patient mother, Yakat. Mother orca are very indulgent with their babies. They appear relaxed, and orca mothering looks effortless, but if mum turns a corner and can no longer hear the sounds of her littlest child, she will turn quickly and rush back, calling until the frisky youngster catches up.

living holding its breath would have a large brain as a luxury feature. Brains are for the storage of experiences, of thoughts, of culture. Every now and then some of the southern resident whales make a trip up Burrard Inlet. Undoubtedly, that body of water was the winter haven for some lineage of orca. Are the whales checking to see if Vancouver is still there? Do they have a memory of "before"?

In November 2002 Nicola's daughter, Tsitika, came through the Broughton. That was the first time I had heard her voice in nine years. She came back a week later, and then close relatives came the week after that. Had she told them the coast was clear, that there were no painful sounds anymore? Does she remember the course her mother travelled through here? Does she know that April is when the feast is spread in Kingcome, that the chum used to end the season in October? What kind of new orca traditions might be forged here in the inlets that once belonged to Eve?

The orca's eye is beneath the leading edge of their eye-patch. The swell of their forehead is an instrument to focus sound and a cushion that protects their enormous and fragile brain.

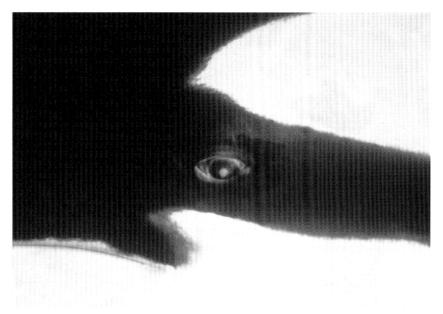

While vision is not the orca's primary sense, they see very well and often look above the water's surface in places where their sophisticated acoustic sonar does not work.

Two young orca play as they travel up Knight Inlet in the glacial meltwater. Every spring the inlets turn a lighter colour as the temperature rises.

The orca is built for speed and mobility. The tall, straight fin acts as a rudder, making it easy for the whale to maintain course. As for why this fin becomes so large on the males, leading orca researcher Dr. Mike Bigg quipped, "It is only because the girls like it."

Top left: A raven surveys his territory. Keen-eyed and very intelligent, he keeps an eye on me in my office. Though he tolerated my presence even while I was noisily chopping wood, it took weeks to get him to allow me to raise a camera lens toward him.

Top right: A northern phalarope pecks at larval organisms on the surface of the plankton layer. Many marine fish and shelled creatures must take a risk-filled tour at the surface; this feeds the ecosystem and gives the young a chance to disperse out of areas already utilized by their parents. In the early years, I tried to find out what kind of fish the phalaropes were eating, and since I couldn't see the tiny larval shrimp, I called them "nothing peckers." Years later, I learned to see what they were actually looking for.

Bottom: A kingfisher balances on a salmon farm, eyeing all the fish held within.

Local Wildlife

Eventually, of course, we realized that other creatures shared the sea with the orca we were studying with such concentration. We began to look around, and our interest in our "neighbourhood" broadened.

Bald eagles have preferred perches from which they survey the richest areas of their territories. These perches are different, depending on what the eagle is hunting: herring in the spring, pink salmon in summer and gulls and diving ducks in winter.

Mystified Ravens and Intrepid Hummingbirds

Ah, the full bloom of spring is a welter of perfectly orchestrated life! The predawn is a symphony of birds — songbirds, Arctic loons, western grebes, common loons, ravens and kingfishers dominate the soundscape. It is impossible to sleep with so many birds excited about the coming day. The scent of the cottonwood drifts enticingly out over the water on the afternoon breeze. There is really nothing like that smell, a tonic of eternal spring and hope. It deeply fills a person's chest, sparks a sigh of happiness.

The ravens know that we humans spawn every year in late March or early April at the Proctors' homestead. They know it is about the same time as the herring spawn, and the blue heron colony returns to the rookery. They watch as we collect in our Easter plumage, then disperse throughout the rough-hewn property to hide our multicoloured eggs. They know the eggs laid on the flats are easy to find, while the ones on the stump-covered hillside are more difficult.

Often the ravens don't see the point of waiting their turn and hop awkwardly behind the smallest children, who are also intent on raiding the newly sighted nests. With brilliant eggs wedged in their jet-black beaks, the ravens make off to their own nests, thinking, perhaps, "How there got to be so many of this creature is astonishing, when they don't even protect their eggs from their own young!" I am sure we mystify many creatures!

Mink are opportunistic and have successfully adapted to living around humans. Here a mink climbs aboard a plank under the ferry dock in Sointula, on Malcolm Island.

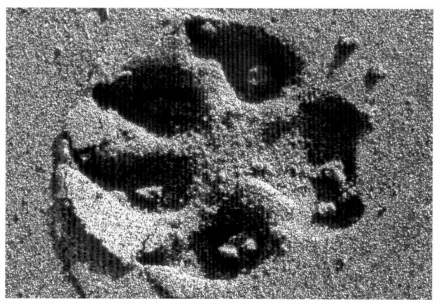

A wolf has left her track in the wet sand of a tiny islet.

Among the most social creatures on the coast, crows travel in mobs, taking advantage of food resources both natural and man-made. Here a young crow sits out a rainstorm, checking out the possibilities in my garden.

As the salmonberry bushes bloom, tiny hummingbirds appear, touching slender beaks to the brilliant pink. They arrive in Bella Bella only three days after appearing in Echo Bay. I shiver at the thought of a tiny hummer setting out from north Vancouver Island to cross Queen Charlotte Strait. Bill and Donna McKay, on the whale-watching vessel *Naiad*, encountered one out on that broad expanse of water.

"We were out in a big westerly," reported Donna, "when a hummingbird appeared at the window and hovered at 26 knots as I stood watch for logs, in the middle of nowhere and then was gone."

A zillion wing-beats to cross the strait? Two zillion in a strong headwind?

A bald eagle banks before a dive. The descent must be perfectly executed at high speed, so that the eagle can snatch a fish and lift it up without crashing into the sea.

Superb spear-fishermen, blue herons have their favourite fishing holes. They alight, crouch and wait motionless for shiner perch and salmon smolts to wander into range. Then, with the speed of lightning, the long neck uncoils and the beak snaps firmly down on the slick fish.

Bonaparte's gulls sunbathe on kelp growing around Pym Rock in Fife Sound.

Gulls lift lazily from the estuary of the Ahta River, the most southerly virgin watershed on the coast. These birds are recovering from the rigours of parenting by feeding on spawned-out salmon carcasses, an essential food source to prepare them for winter.

A male (left) and female
Steller's sea lion rest, warming
themselves in the last rays of
the setting sun. Sea lions use
very few places to haul out
on the central coast. This is a
winter site on the outer edge
of the Broughton Archipelago.

Harbour seals are not well
armed to defend themselves,
and their fat bodies make a
good food source for transient
orca as well as land-based
predators. As a result, they
are extremely wary, easily
awakened from naps. Most
often they sleep only in the
low-tide zone, avoiding the
forest's edge.

Steller's sea lions lounge on their rock overlooking Queen Charlotte Strait. While in alarming decline in Alaska, sea lions are still thriving here in B.C.

A Skiing Spider

One day as I was cruising around in my boat, I noticed a strange, single, V-shaped ripple. Little salmon swim in groups of tens to hundreds, but this was a lone ripple. I idled my boat slowly closer. It isn't easy to glimpse wild, free-swimming salmon because they are very attuned to predators from above, such as kingfishers and blue herons.

As I got closer I realized it was a spider water-skiing! A tiny yellow spider had its two back legs braced apart and set delicately on the water's surface, creating a pair of dimples. While the spider's back feet etched two slipstream wakes, its front legs were hanging on to the long arch of a single strand of web that reached into the sky. The breeze was too minute for me to feel, but it caught the spider's sail and this brave arachnid was on a voyage to new lands. You never know what you'll see in the waters of this Earth.

A humpback whale raises her flukes as she tilts into a steep dive to hunt herring in Knight Inlet.

Other Whales

My main research focus was on marine mammals, and when the orca disappeared from the Broughton Archipelago because of the AHDs on the salmon farms, I turned my attention to dolphins and other species of whales.

A plump Pacific white-sided dolphin leaps ahead of my boat in Fife Sound. These dolphins began appearing on the British Columbia coast in 1984 after an absence of about a human lifetime. My research has shown that they probably move inshore every 30 to 70 years to feed on the shoals of pilchard, anchovies and capelin that pulse in and out on the same cycles.

Humpback Whales

Humpback whales used to live in the Broughton Archipelago year-round. According to longtime fishermen, there were about seven in Knight Inlet, three or four in Kingcome Inlet and two in Fife Sound. People had names for the two in Fife: Barney (for a barnacle on his head) and The Missus. Sometimes the whales scratched themselves on the underside of the floathouses, and one man remembers rowing up to a sleeping humpback and touching it. In 1952 the whaler *Nahmint* came around northern Vancouver Island from Coal Harbour to kill the whales of the Broughton. They were easy targets, being used to humans and their boats. There had been many inshore populations of humpback whales in

British Columbia, but each was taken by the whalers, one after the other. Coal Harbour was the last whaling station in B.C. and it closed in 1968.

Humpback whales were not spotted in this area again until December 1980. In 1986 we photo-identified two in Knight Inlet. While orca are identified by their dorsal fins and the saddle behind the dorsal, humpbacks are identified by the underside of their flukes. How does a researcher get a picture of the underside of a whale's tail? By waiting patiently for it to raise its flukes out of the water before making a deep dive.

We have identified 10 humpback whales that now use the archipelago, some of which return every year. Two have brought their babies with them. Iwama comes in March for herring. Maude brought her baby Galen, but never returned after the salmon farms began using AHDs on her summer feeding ground, Greenway Sound. Houdini came for the pilchard when they returned and then came back with her baby too. Phantom had a blow so loud it could be heard for miles.

The return of the humpback whale to the inshore waters of British Columbia is a sign of hope and a lesson that conservation can work to bring species back from the brink of extinction.

This unfortunate gray whale died off Echo Bay, emaciated and bearing fresh wounds of an orca attack. Dead whales speak volumes, revealing the trials of their lives. Gray whales are bottom feeders, sifting through sand for their food, but this whale made the mistake of scooping up fragments of wood underneath a log-booming ground. In her belly were bales of wood fibre so tightly compacted that they may have caused her death.

Minke whales, the smallest of the baleen whales, feed on herring along the outer reaches of the archipelago. When they blow, their breath smells strongly of herring. They are fast and very beautiful with their lovely streaks of grey.

The head of a humpback whale, as shown here, looks prehistoric. Each bump harbours a hair, thought to give the whale information about vibrations caused by fish movements. The blowhole is visible, an inverted V on the top of the head.

This species of barnacle, Cryptolepas rhachianecti, *is found only on gray whales.*

Baleen from a gray whale. There are toothed whales and baleen whales. A baleen whale engulfs large amounts of seawater, then closes its mouth, leaving only the baleen exposed, and pushes the water back out with its tongue. The food is trapped behind the baleen.

Two humpback whales, which I named Silver and Nick, in Knight Inlet.

Three dolphins race alongside my boat in Queen Charlotte Strait. They are generally an early sign of fall. The high-speed play exhibited by dolphins tells us they are on an abundant, high-calorie diet. Keeping a body warm in the cold North Pacific takes energy, and having enough energy to play as well means that these dolphins are making a good living here.

"Popcorning" is a behaviour that occurs frequently in the fall when the dolphins arrive and is often associated with sex. Several dolphins leap into the air at once, and all appear to try to get back into the water at the same spot.

Part of my dolphin research is figuring out who swims with whom, in an effort to understand their communities. I started naming them, but now that I have almost a thousand identified, I have reverted to using numbers. This is a coalition of males. These all-male groups patrol through most large assemblies of dolphins.

Harbour Porpoise

While some events, like seeing a humpback, can be relatively rare, others are so common they aren't noticed. The surfacing of a harbour porpoise is like that. Harbour porpoise live closer to people on a regular basis than any other whale, dolphin or porpoise. This is not because they like us or benefit from our often-sloppy ways, but because we both thrive in the same habitat — shallow water, near land. There are two kinds of porpoise resident on the coast of British Columbia — the Dall porpoise and the harbour porpoise — and they have a pact that keeps them from competing with each other. The Dalls use the deep, more open waters, and the harbours stay closer to the beach. In the Broughton, Dalls are rare occasional visitors in spring and fall, while harbour porpoise live right off the end of my float and throughout the waterways of the archipelago year-round.

I remember a neighbour radioing me one time, "Alex, there's a new kind of dolphin just off my floathouse. You might want to come and take a look." I dashed over expectantly, only to find the woman pointing excitedly at the harbour porpoise that had been living there for years. There is something about these porpoise that simply slips beneath our radar; they are generally too understated for us to notice.

Full-grown harbour porpoise reach about five feet and a hundred pounds. They have a rounded triangular fin, with no hint of the sickle shape characteristic to dolphins. They are a mousy-gray on top, white beneath and delicately streaked between the face and throat. We don't really know how long they live; some say 8 years, others 15, and still others suspect they live much longer.

I see newborns from June through August. They are tiny footballs, shadowing their mother's every move. Baby cetaceans typically swim just behind the widest point of their mother's body, right behind the dorsal fin. Tucked in behind the outward curve of mum's ribs, the little ones surf a back eddy. I have seen baby dolphins with their eyes shut thus cradled by the flow of water along their mother's body. I suspect the mother and youngster off my float every day are the same individuals, but I don't know for sure. This is probably their foreshore, perhaps in their family for years, decades or centuries.

While harbour porpoise are declining around southern Vancouver Island, they are still abundant in the Broughton Archipelago and are a common meal for the mammal-eating orca. When chased, the porpoise sometimes streak away to

Often one dolphin will leap out of the water and hit the surface with its belly 20 to 30 times in a row. While this might be a form of communication, it might also be a way to herd fish or dominate other group members.

shallow water. The large male orca can't get close to them, seemingly burdened by their enormous dorsal and pectoral fins, but the smaller females and teenagers keep pace with the porpoise. I've seen them tearing along white clamshell beaches: "*Pfffft, pfffft,*" blow the porpoise, followed by the "*KWOOOOOOF*" of the whale. As they approach the end of the beach, the porpoise turn on a dime and head away from shore and, more often than not, are met by the male contingent of the orca family.

A kayak is the perfect vessel from which to observe harbour porpoise. Look along the tidelines of the narrow passes of the archipelago. They are not shy, just no-nonsense, and if you are lucky you might see them flash beneath your boat for a split second before they vanish again.

Dolphins

The dolphins are here in winter in groups of hundreds with lots of babies. It took over 10 years for the mothers with young babies to come into the archipelago, and now they are not only here but they're also allowing the babies to play with the boats. The little fellows rocket about with astonishing speed. Most days are too rough and stormy for me to join them, but it is good to know they can make a living here again. Their careless, noisy, fun-loving nature is evident as they race about, leaping in trios and quartets, but I know they are always on the watch for the transient whales that would eat them, and they stage their play directly above the schools of pollock, herring and other fish species that sustain them. They are not as random as they appear.

Here a dolphin rides the bow wave of my boat. We may be the only species which takes delight in this behaviour. Humpback whales and orca become quite annoyed when the pesky dolphins cluster about their "bow waves." One dolphin delight is sex, under my boat at 25 knots!

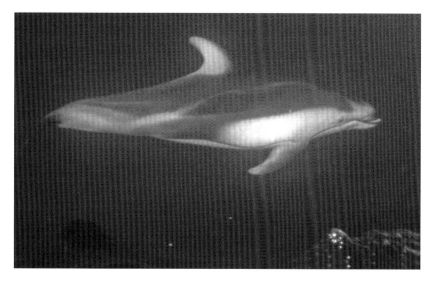

In the crystal-clear winter sea of the Broughton a dolphin glides effortlessly alongside my boat. These dolphins are very curious and will approach and inspect every vessel plying their waters.

A humpback breaching in Knight Inlet. For reasons unknown, humpbacks often breach many times in a row during brisk westerly winds. A long-time resident of the area told me that her school boat could not get into Simoom Sound one day because of the exuberant breaching of several humpbacks.

Pacific white-sided dolphins arrive in the fall and depart in late spring on a schedule opposite to the orca. Here a threesome plays in Queen Charlotte Strait. The dolphins' relentless play bespeaks a large-brained intelligence and successful lifestyle, with time permitted for pleasure.

A pilchard in Echo Bay.

Fish

Most marine mammals live on fish, and I began to understand that every creature, however tiny or insignificant, fills a niche in the food chain in the ocean.

❦

Pilchard

On an August morning in 1997 I was skimming over calm seas headed west in Fife Sound. The morning was coloured with a delicate palette of pinks and silvery greys, and I was leaning out the window to drink in the fresh scent of sea and forest when I noticed a school of fish flash beneath me. Pink salmon, I wondered? Then another and another school materialized in a kaleidoscope of scattering shapes. I slowed my boat and turned back, curious.

As I looked for another school of these fish, I noticed a patch of finely rippled water. Heading toward it, I could just make out hundreds of fish travelling with their mouths agape, grazing the surface, creating the ripples. The fish wouldn't let me close enough to see them clearly, and I spiralled for

Oolichan freshly caught from the Franklin River at the head of Knight Inlet fry onboard Billy Proctor's fishboat Twilight Rock. *No fish tastes better!*

hours trying different methods of getting a good look. The sheer number of these fish represented a significant addition to the archipelago, and I wanted to know what they were. A friend passing by in his boat saw me going in circles, thought the steering had broken in my boat and radioed me: "Do you need help?"

I was wondering if the archipelago had suddenly been invaded by the voracious schools of mackerel that were infiltrating B.C. waters on warm water currents and feeding on young salmon. I had never seen a mackerel. The next morning my neighbour, Pat Ordano, radioed to say she had heard me talking about the strange schools of fish and that her husband, Gary, had just caught one. Did I want to

A school of herring. Most of the marine predators of the coast, from chinook salmon to humpback whales, depend on this energy-rich fish.

take a look at it? I gathered all the fish-identification books I could find and went to have a look. On the way, more schools flashed beneath the boat. There were a lot of these fish, whatever they were!

As we tied to Pat's dock, she brought coffee, cookies for my daughter, Clio, and one of the most beautiful little fish I have ever seen. It was about 10 inches long, highly cylindrical with large, overlapping scales. It was deep metallic blue-green on top, lightening to silver along the belly. The side of its head was marked with a pattern like raindrops flowing down a pane of glass, and big black spots formed rows along its side. I had no idea what it was, but looking through the book I could see it was not the dreaded mackerel. In fact, there was no picture in any of my books that matched this fish.

A few days later a little boy caught a strange fish off the wharf in Port McNeill, which no one recognized until an old-timer came along and with disbelief exclaimed, "That's a pilchard!" He hadn't seen one for 50 years.

Pilchard is a local name for sardines. They are related to herring and spawn off California. Each year of their life they migrate north and then south again to California, pressing a little farther north each year of their lives. They eat plankton, diatoms and copepods. When I saw them swimming with mouths open at the surface, they were straining these organisms out of the water. Through the 1920s and '30s pilchard were an important fishery in British Columbia with the highest catch in 1929 at 86,300 tons. Most of this was rendered into oil and meal. The oil was extracted and used in making soaps and shortening and the meal was food for chickens, although canned pilchard is an excellent human food. In 1939 the fishery began to crash and by 1945 it was over. No one had reported seeing a pilchard since 1950. Fortunately for this generation of pilchard, no one is now allowed to render edible fish into fish meal in Canada.

A few weeks after the wonderful discovery that pilchard were in the archipelago, I was trying to get an identification photograph of a humpback whale. I had named this humpback whale Houdini, because she had an uncanny ability to disappear. As I drifted in my boat with the engine off, trying to detect the sound of the whale's blow, a school of pilchard appeared and flowed with unimaginable grace just beneath the water's surface. Like one living organism, the school wound a serpentine course, sometimes spiralling inward through itself. They positively did not like a shadow and split at my boat, flowing around me only to knit back together on the other side. Rich in oil, these fish represented a wealth of energy and calories in a cold northern sea. Then without warning, a monolithic flash of brilliant pink erupted

A school of spawning pink salmon lies dark and massive in the Ahta River in August.

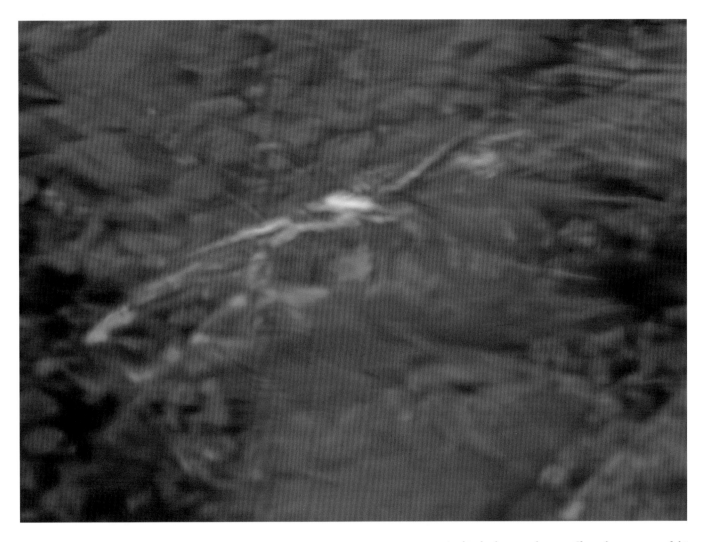

A dead chum salmon offers the success of his life to future generations. Energy is finite and is carefully recycled in the natural world.

A large, toothy chum salmon moves upriver to find a mate, dig a nest, spawn and die, to feed perhaps a bear, an eagle, a raven and hundreds of insects.

A mass of shellfish eggs blooms in the intertidal zone in mid-spring.

right beside me. Water gushed in a cascading waterfall and fish were propelled into the air, their scales blinding flashes of sunlight. I must have jumped because I fell off my seat onto the hard floor in the shock of surprise. It was Houdini having dinner and I was floating in the midst of the main course. I saw her close her maw and force the rest of the water out of her mouth through her baleen. She sank and a moment later all was silent again. From then on I moved away from the schools of pilchard if I thought a humpback whale was nearby.

The harbour seals were on a learning curve as they figured out how to encircle a school of pilchard and then rise beneath the fish. The pilchard responded in a spectacular bid to become airborne, creating the exact sound of a whale's blow — *whooooosh*. I got fooled many times and raced down to the docks only to scan fruitlessly for a whale, ignoring the little seal looking back at me.

On an August afternoon the following summer, I passed a shallow bay and spied the now-familiar pattern of tiny ripples moving across the water. As I idled in, I was treated to the memorable vision of a school of pilchard flowing through the sinuous green of a kelp forest. I lifted Clio to the window, "Look, baby, there's one of the wonders of the world." I had no idea when I started my study of whales in 1984 that the archipelago would offer such epic spectacles of the rhythms of life.

Spring

Spring in the Broughton is a spectacle to behold. The hooded nudibranchs once again meet, making flowers of eggs on the rocks in their designated bays. Is that where the current takes them or do they struggle relentlessly against tide and current to reach it? Their luminescent opal forms billow and wave as they cluster.

Algal blooms multiply and fade in rapid succession. With a few days of sun, the water becomes rich with the food that young salmon, herring and oolichan require to grow rapidly out of their most vulnerable stage. Several days of rain and cloud, and the water clears; the stage is set for the next burst of energy from the sun.

The starfish have been on their tiptoes for weeks, releasing spawn from between their many legs, tentacles caressing each other. The barnacles and mussels have covered all available surfaces with tiny replicas of themselves, their success as species confirmed on the bottom of every boat that plies these waters.

It isn't easy to be a baby in the spring sea. Over a period of three weeks a dark centre materializes within the clear herring eggs. A flicker of movement can be seen, then the water is filled with fish the width of a human hair, wriggling in prolific abandon. They feed on life so minute it takes a herring's eye or a microscope to see. Then they align and move before the pantry empties. Swim and grow, swim and

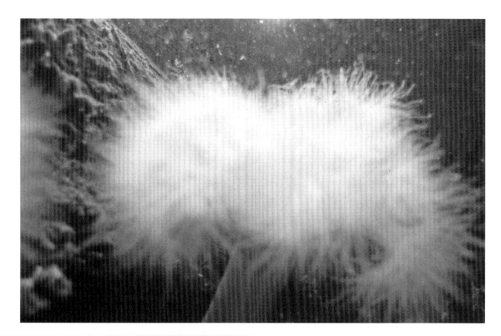

My downstairs neighbours: giant plumose anemones, attached to logs under my floathouse.

A butter clam with a hole neatly drilled through its shell by a moon snail.

The spiny dogfish is a shark. Small, with rough, sandpapery teeth, this species is not a threat to humans but feeds on herring and other fish.

grow. As the clouds of herring swirl west along steep-sided inlet shores, they mingle and ripple through the silver shoals of salmon.

First the jailbird-striped little chums leave the sweet fresh water and change their bodies to meet the salt. Where they meet Tribune Channel, the composition of the schools changes and the pure silver of the pinks dominates. In every dent on the coast these 2.5- to 4-cm recently born fish rest and feed. Unlike the coho, also hatching at this time, the chums and pinks do not take refuge in shallow, cedar-swept river pools. The pinks and chums are unique among the salmonids of this planet in that they do not use the rivers to feed their young; they move out to sea as fry.

There they are met by a terrifying array of predators. Coho in their second year, now in the sea, feed so voraciously on the baby pinks that the margin between survival and collapse of every broodyear is but a sliver. The only passage through this phase is rapid growth, so they interrupt their ocean migration to swallow everything they see. Sea lice also attack. Tiny brown copepods bore into the tender flesh of baby salmon, attach and grow, sucking life juices out of these fish, the coast's tiny couriers of essential energy. Some of these fish are so young their yolk sacs are still visible. Pink fry with lice cannot gain weight and remain too long in the most dangerous phase of their life, as coho food. The ocean is full of threats for little ones.

Herring

The archipelago hums a soft, sweet song in spring. It is hard to hear in February — more an expectation than a full-fledged rhythm — but on my hydrophone, just before the first light of dawn, I can hear them coming. Their voices are ripe with life, their swishing juicy, like the sound of a lemon squeezed above a salmon. It is the sound of tons of herring coming home to spawn.

As vast as a herd of caribou or wildebeest, herring on the move can be easily missed from topside. But no biomass this immense can pass unnoticed if you recognize their sign upon the sea. On the cusp of dawn and dark the fish move up and down. At night they rise to feed on surface plankton layers, at dawn they dive to escape the beaks of birds and teeth of dolphins, and their air bladders must adjust. Billions of tiny bubbles are released on these vertical migrations and produce a distinctive sheen on the water's surface. These are the "footprints" of the gift of life, an immeasurable fecundity that turns the inlets of this coast on — one by one in northerly progression.

Herring, like salmon, feed the masses in their act of procreation. Unlike us mammals, who must hide away our rare and precious young, the herring cast them upon the sea in huge numbers that they hope will be too great for even the greedy who gather. The moon calls these fish. Herring can feel the ebb and flood grow larger, building to the full-moon tides of March, and this is when they spawn. Historically, herring spawned over 258 kilometres of coastline, but today they use much smaller, specific sites. Scientists wonder if there are simply no elders among the herring to lead younger generations to the old places.

As tiny as a herring sperm is, so much is released by these spectacular males that the shorelines blanch white and opaque. The eggs adhere to the seaweed in layers so thick it looks like snow when the tide recedes. The gulls, hungry from the winter months, paddle contentedly along these drifts. Peck and swallow is all they need to do now to regain their prime condition.

Seals and dolphins escort the herring. Chinook salmon swirl in bronzy, lethal flashes, storing a richness they will later bestow upon the forests high above the tidal mark when they spawn later in the year. In turn the Steller's sea lions follow the salmon and herring. The orca of A pod arrive as well, to feed on the herring-filled chinook salmon. Eagles clasp talons full of herring, eating them in mid-air to ease the hunger pangs of winter. As I hear the swishing song of herring on my hydrophone, I expect Iwama, the humpback I call "the March whale." Tasting the herring from unknown distances away, this whale has made an appointment in his whale-sized mental date book: "North Cramer Pass, March — be there." Then he'll vanish to the next location stored carefully in his mind.

Herring require two to four years to mature. They don't die after spawning and can produce increasing numbers of eggs, up to 38,000 annually by their eighth year. In an ocean allowed to continue its natural processes, the fish return year after year, leading the youngsters to the places where herring eggs can still survive. There is no better time than spring. The whispers of the herring vanish with the rising sun, but they will be back tomorrow; for this place, theirs is the song of life. Where there is herring, there is hope.

Herring eggs frost the Fucus seaweed that thrives in the Broughton Archipelago.

Salmon

The more I followed whales, the more I wanted to know about salmon, because they have such influence over the whales' movements. Different species of animals attract our attention for different reasons. Pandas appear cute, elephants wise, snakes frightening, horses noble and whales magnificent. As I spent more time in Johnstone Strait, I became attracted to salmon for their sheer generosity. In August millions of sockeye funnel through Blackney and Weyton passes into Johnstone Strait en route to their rivers to spawn. The abundance of these fish is astonishing. At times there were fish leaping in the air as far as the eye could see across the strait and to the east and west. Their silver sides shimmered and glinted over the dark waters.

Salmon are a benevolent species. From the moment the translucent pink eggs leave their mothers' bodies, they sustain the life around them, beginning with fresh-water trout, birds and insects. During their life at sea the vast shoals of silver salmon feed sharks, dolphins and many other species. As eggs and sperm ripen, inner signals steer the fish home. Miraculously, salmon can find the exact stretch of gravel they were spawned in, probably by taste.

There are five species of salmon on the west coast of North America. While they all incubate in the clean gravel of clear, cold streams, travel out to sea to feed and then return to their exact birthplace to spawn, each species has evolved unique characteristics. Each species selects slightly different habitat for spawning — gravel of different sizes, stream flow of varying speeds, lakes, glacial meltwater, deep pools or shallow riffles, etc. — to ensure maximum production from every creek. The consecutive annual runs of each species ebb and surge to give the rivers a rest. Then each spring millions of young salmon head out into the Pacific. Kingfishers, mergansers and blue herons feed the tiny salmon to their nestlings.

Salmon reproduce at spectacular levels, far beyond their own needs. That nature can transform the richness of the Pacific Ocean into the succulent flesh of a salmon shows her at her best. That the forces of nature drive the fish to transport that richness through coastal waters, inland and up into the Rocky Mountains is a supreme gift to every ecosystem along the way.

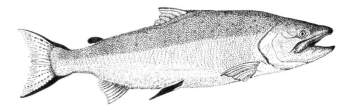

Oolichan

Oh, the oolichan. They swim unseen, a secret much anticipated along this coast. "Will they show or won't they?" is the question in many First Nations villages all spring. Then — *shazam!* — they will rise from depths to enter the swift icy waters of the Kingcome River. These fish are not slippery like herring or salmon. They are a member of the smelt family and can easily be grabbed as they lie in eddies in the rocky, cobble bottom of the river. The eagles know this and their brilliant white heads twinkle like stars against the dark-green hillsides above an oolichan spawn. The fish manage to stick their eggs to smooth, eons-worn rocks in the spring freshets of their rivers. The eagles use the fish to provide the calories they require to enter their season of raising eaglets.

Oolichan are so rich in oil that the dried fish was burned by First Nations people as a source of light. The tribes that lived near oolichan-spawning grounds rendered the fish down to a strong-smelling oil or "grease" as they call it. This oil provided essential nutrients to a people faced with cold, wet conditions, and the grease became a major trade article.

*Sword ferns flourish on the nitrogen brought from
the open Pacific Ocean by the incoming salmon.*

Plant Life

Salmon feed the forest as well as marine creatures. Trees and other plants depend on the nutrients brought back from the open ocean by the salmon returning to spawn; their bodies provide fertilizer for ongoing life in many forms.

⟦❦⟧

The Salmon Forest

The rich product of millions of square miles of surface ocean photosynthesis is stored in the pink flesh of the Pacific salmon. They feed whales, sea lions, eagles and human communities as they surge home in pulses from June through November, and then in a most extraordinary interweaving of life, they carry ocean energy up into the coastal mountains as they return to spawn.

The size of salmon runs can actually be read from the width of growth rings in trees: if the run is small, the rings will be narrow; if there is a large return, the rings will be wide and generous. The bears, wolves, ravens, and other species contribute to this process by dragging spawned-out salmon

Western dock, growing on the Ahta River estuary. This useful plant is the antidote for nettle stings.

carcasses deep into the forest as they fatten up to survive the winter. In return, the trees cool the streams with their canopy and meter out the rainfall, preventing flash floods and mudslides from killing the salmon. The phosphorus from pink salmon has been found in the flesh of mountain goats on peak-crowning glaciers. The salmon carcasses left in and near the river feed the insects that will nourish the young salmon that emerge from the gravel the following spring. If the salmon runs are lost, the entire forest will be diminished.

Salmon feed the forest and the forest in turn provides sanctuary for the salmon's young.

Huckleberries twinkle their tart goodness in the September sun, food for bears, birds and humans alike. This prosperous bush has its roots in the river and its solar panels (its leaves) reaching for the sun over the open water.

False lily-of-the-valley loves the forest floor under old-growth spruce trees.

*Moonrise over the forest
of Johnstone Strait.*

*A Douglas aster blows gaily in a summer
breeze from the Wakeman Valley.*

The Brassica group (Brussels sprouts, kale, broccoli) thrives in coastal gardens, weathering both frost and heavy rain to feed us all year long.

Bunchberry grows close to the forest floor wherever sunlight penetrates the canopy.

A cultivated tulip shows off the beauty of sea urchin shells, opened carefully for a meal of urchin roe.

*Commercial salmon boats anchor on the best fishing spots, awaiting an opening.
The orca get to fish first, as the fishing crews take pictures of them. Many whales
used to be shot because they were seen as competition for salmon. Today fishermen
are much more tolerant of the whales.*

Fishing

Of course, salmon and other fish feed humans too. Fishing is an important way of life along the coast.

❧

Up the Wakeman River

As we bounced up the valley in Steve Vesly's old pickup, I glimpsed the Wakeman River through the trees. She lay smooth and unhurried, a liquid serpent. Her head was sleeping among the frozen glacial fields, her tail sweeping lazily among the swans wintering in her estuary. At a break in the forest we stopped, and Steve, wiry and strong at nearly 70 years old, hauled the raft out of his truck as if it were nothing. From there the two young men I was accompanying on this trip gingerly threaded the inflatable through the brush and set it in a small back eddy. Bristling with cameras, I followed, excited to finally be rafting the Wakeman. Some years 700,000 pink salmon, 4,000 coho, 18,000 chum and 1,000 chinook spawn in this river and her tributaries. Historic numbers were undoubtedly much, much larger.

One "pull" on the Twilight Rock off Triangle Island some years ago yielded all five species of salmon: pink, sockeye, coho, chum and chinook.

Seine nets rise out of the water and onto a fishboat in Blackfish Sound.

I could see every pebble and submerged log in a river that generally runs milky white with silt. It was still too cold in the mountains for the glaciers to begin melting and bathe the river in its summer plumage. The water level was low and the Wakeman's ribs were showing, pebbly ridges breaking the surface in places. The lumbering raft sprang to life in the water, and we began our seaward migration.

As the fishermen weighed the possibilities of using gooey bobs, Colorado swivelers, perhaps a pink worm and other such cryptic things, I explored. The riverbank was fine white sand. The single trilling note of the varied thrush sounded, dream-like, from the leafing forest. Wolf tracks were pressed deep into the clean sand — a large one and a much smaller one. A marten's tracks traversed the pair and the spindly toes of a raven paraded alongside.

I have never fished in a river, but I know the sound of line peeling off a reel. I rummaged in my backpack for a camera: video, black and white, colour? As I mused, I was reprimanded.

"Put those things AWAY! Don't you know it's bad luck to take a camera out before a fish is landed?"

Shoulda known, fishermen have so many superstitions — lucky caps, bad-luck days, don't open a can of milk upside down, don't leave a pail of water on deck, don't take a woman fishing. They were all reasons why the big one got away, but I obliged and zipped up the bag.

Billy Proctor, lifelong fisherman and resident of the Broughton Archipelago, mends his gillnet, his hands weathered by his years at sea.

Fishing in a home-built skiff on the edge of Queen Charlotte Strait.

A troller. Fishermen hold a wealth of information about our oceans, and much of my research depends on them. As highly successful fish predators, they know a great deal about the species they pursue, and many of them are keen conservationists.

A very good day fishing on the troller Twilight Rock. These sockeye have been cleaned and are awaiting the second wash before being laid on ice in the hold.

"Feels like a 12-pound Atlantic buck!"

That's right — we were hunting Atlantic salmon in this Pacific watershed. My friends had landed six the day before, but the instinct of today's river fishermen to release all fish was so deep in them that they'd let them go. I, however, wanted those escaped farm fish OUT of this river and that

My smokehouse full of oolichan. A member of the smelt family, this little fish was crucial to the traditional First Nations economy as a major trade item.

was why we were on the Wakeman. They caught two more and then lost one that could have been 18 to 20 pounds. Guess I jinxed that one as I got it on video. We never saw a wild fish at all. The two bucks had teeth marks made by other fish etched cross-hatched on their bodies. They were living up to their reputation — aggressive.

The Atlantics were lying in the pools the Wakeman's wild progeny would soon cross. Each tiny fry would stand out in silhouette to feed the Atlantics we didn't take that day. The farm fish were fit enough to be here, fit enough to fight with the other fish in the pool and fit enough to bite lures designed for wild fish. Their scrambled DNA — some farmer's dream — might see them through only enough life history to disrupt the salmon empire built by the natural forces of this coast. Norwegian scientists have estimated that if only 30% of a spawning population in a stream are escaped Atlantics, the native salmon stock can be rendered extinct.

As I rode down the reaches of Kingcome Inlet later that day in my speedboat, the words of a top-level Fisheries bureaucrat rang in my head: "In my view it is only a matter of time before we discover that Atlantics are gaining a foothold in B.C."

The rich flavour of oolichan beckons to all, even Mocha, my Jack Russell terrier, who generally prefers her fish cooked.

Catching a few oolichan for dinner, Billy Proctor waits poised on the banks of the Franklin River at the head of Knight Inlet.

A petroglyph. This carved stone face rests, chin deep, on a beach near the north end of Vancouver Island.

People

People have lived in this richly nourishing area for thousands of years, in much greater numbers than today. Their art reminds us that the First Nations did not interrupt the flow of life, even though they themselves lived very well.

European pioneers like the Hallidays began to arrive on the central coast in the early 20th century; now modern settlers make their living here in many different ways.

≈

Rain

Though most of my photographs show sunny weather, it *does* rain here on the coast, and the fall of 2001 was especially moist. Rain on the hydrophone, rain on the roof, rain, rain and more rain down my back. It was starting to feel like "40 days and 40 nights." I thought six inches in August was wet, but we were over 11 inches for October with one more week to go. Everyone had to bail out their boats twice a day just to stay afloat. "Felt like I was under a waterfall," quipped my neighbour Billy Proctor, describing his dash to get his boat

A totem pole standing in Kingcome village.

away from the dock in a fierce westerly gale one night. We got an inch and a half that night. Then the wind switched to southeast and it *really* began to rain.

You can usually tell a local from a tourist, because locals never wear raingear. I don't know why — I guess you just get used to being damp — but that fall I broke down and bought a raincoat. Damp is fine, soaked isn't. It rained so hard the children had to wear life jackets just to cross the puddles. I saw cormorants trying to "dry" their wings in a mere shower, and my chickens demanded room service; when I opened their door they stared at me in disbelief, "What do you think we are, ducks?"

Rain is what built this coast to its historic abundance. Rain allowed First Nations people to live here in higher density than any other hunting-gathering society on Earth. While the precipitation looked overwhelming, the ecosystem had clearly seen it before and took advantage. Young trees had 18 inches of new growth; pink salmon, which usually spawn near the estuaries, were sighted farther up the watersheds than ever before; and toad abundance in my muddy garden was at a record high. I used to encourage my soggy-spirited neighbours by reminding them that all the water falling from the sky was good for the fish, but I stopped.

It rained so hard I never heard the annual flyby of the southern migration of sandhill cranes. I thought I heard whales calling one night but couldn't be sure over the roar

An orca tops a totem pole at Mi'mkwamlis village on Village Island.

This totem pole, on Village Island south of Knight Inlet, has now fallen and is returning to the earth, an organic art form replenishing the soil.

of a billion drops of water all crashing into the sea at once. How do whales breathe in rain, their blowholes open as potholes to the pelting water? Does the outward blast of their exhale dry a pocket of air for one nanosecond? Or were they coughing water out?

Alright already, enough about the weather! But it was more than weather; it could be a regime shift and to anyone studying Earth's natural workings, that's exciting. Anomaly or not, that was the question, and I found it fascinating. Depraved, perhaps; wet definitely; but happily so.

Pictographs at the head of Kingcome show the cattle that still range wild there, descendants of those that escaped from the Hallidays, the first Europeans to farm in the inlet.

This pictograph in Tribune Channel may depict a harpooned Steller's sea cow.

A frog carved into a fallen pole at Mi'mkwamlis village.

Adze marks shape a ridge pole at an ancient village site.

A burial box sits untouched and hidden from today's inhabitants of the Broughton Archipelago.

A wooden mallet lies, finally at rest, at the Halliday farm.

Necessity is the mother of invention. Boatbuilder Eric Nelson heats water in an old propane tank by setting it in a wood fire. The steam created is channeled into a wooden box where boards are placed. He can then bend the steamed boards without breaking them and fit them to the curved edge of a boat.

*A tiny floathouse is easy to heat and a perfect dwelling for a bachelor.
Floathouses have been a way of life for over a hundred years in the
Broughton Archipelago, with little effect on the environment.*

Good conversation is a highly rated entertainment in remote areas. Over a cup of coffee, a newly emerging boat is admired by its builder, Eric Nelson, and Dave Parker.

Symbolism: Top Notch surfaces below the pictograph (rock painting) of orca that adorns the entrance to Kingcome Inlet.

Sister orca matriarchs Kelsey and Yakat pass Alert Bay as a resident mows the lawn. Whales and people live contentedly as neighbours here.

Homesteading is one of the most satisfying human experiences. Here, my home alters a piece of land for my family to live on. The house on the right was a floathouse that was pulled up onto land.

Dinner! Fresh fish, new potatoes and greens from the garden are mainstays for coastal dwellers. Living near the fish, with a small area for growing veggies, ensures better food than even the most exclusive city market can provide.

Moving day in a floathouse requires no boxes — only a boat, a strong rope and a secure destination safe from the winter winds. It is astonishing to have the morning light come into a new room with every move and to see a new view from every window.

A road to nowhere. An ancient wooden logging road is reclaimed by the forest in Claydon Bay.

A cedar stump of massive proportions is surrounded by spindly young trees — they are hundreds of years away from recreating the ecosystem in which the big tree fell.

Oolichan smoke in a cedar smokehouse, while a new garden awaits seeds. The gardener appears to have great respect for the ability of the local deer to get over a fence!

Floathouses rise and fall with the tide; they make it easy for people to follow their work and change both neighbours and the scenery. Pictures need constant straightening, and the water in a warm tub sloshes gently.

Echo Bay

Homesteading in Echo Bay is a wonderful way to live. Because there are no roads, we all get around in boats, and whether it's for work or for social occasions, the ocean is the focus of our existence.

❧

Finding Home

Scimitar, matriarch of the A12s, led me into Fife Sound on a cool October day. The place is so beautiful, remote and wild, I felt as if I were travelling into a new dimension. Mist clung to deep green hills, and beneath the water was silence so profound, the whales' voices were all that existed. That day, in my heart, I made Echo Bay my home.

Echo Bay is a micro-community of only 40 people. Most of the houses are on floats, as is the post office. There is a one-room school at the head of the bay; the 10 to 15 children arrive by boat, and the curriculum includes studying life in the tiny creek behind the school. This bay has supported human life for 8,000 years; a broad white beach at the head of it is made of the clam and barnacle shells from a thousand feasts.

When the Vancouver Aquarium shipped me a harbour seal for rehabilitation, the children enthusiastically filled buckets with shiner perch to feed it. The seal learned quickly how to catch these fish it loved so much, and we dubbed them "seal potato chips."

The mail comes in three times a week by seaplane. There are no roads or ferries to or from Echo Bay. The only television signal is by satellite, and the only phones are cell phones. The recent development of two-way satellite Internet has, however, brought Echo Bay into the age of high-speed communication. At Halloween the children trick or treat by boat, and they race the ravens for eggs at the Easter egg hunt. The community consists of fishermen, artists, Department of Fisheries and Oceans patrolmen, homesteaders and one whale researcher. Echo Bay offers an independent life in the wilderness, where children grow up free from the pressures of consumerism, drugs and overcrowded schools.

Children of the coast are drawn to the rich and exciting low-tide zone. Their feet become tough and their balance is superb. Nothing is regular, so one must always look before stepping.

The Importance of Growing Kale

In mid-December Echo Bay is hunkered down, trying to hang onto all of its floating bits. Hurricane south*east*, gale south*west*, storm westerly, then back to the southeast. We prepare for each wind in a different way: tuck in an extra bumper, move boats to another dock, tighten anchor lines, slack off spring lines to allow the boat to rise and fall on cresting seas without ripping the float apart. Our community is built to weather the southeasters. The ducks come into the bay in the south wind because, while gales scream off the hilltops, the water is calm. But the First Nations name for the rocky beach outside the bay, below my garden — "Place where waves beat against rock" — becomes frighteningly apparent in an icy, midnight westerly blow.

Here, there is no clear boundary between the environment and the humans. The wind tries to steal our boats, knocks over clotheslines, carries the scent of our fires out to sea and strums ageless rhythms on hundred-year-old trees. Our puny, hairless, mammalian form is never more vulnerable than in a storm. Should I hide on the float away from falling trees, or on the hill beyond the reach of those black, clawing mountains of water coming up the pass? Which tree is most likely to come down? Where is my house built the strongest? Is anywhere safe? At some point I have to relax, mid-gale, and simply throw my lot in with the life around me. The molecules of this archipelago have mingled

Like salmon, kale is a gift to humanity. This calcium-rich plant grows prolifically on the coast, loving the cool, moist air. In spring it produces tall, succulent stems that I call "Broughton asparagus."

with my human ones, sharing salt, oxygen and water; we are one system.

Yes, we are one system; there is no us and them, no jobs versus the environment, no difference in the air breathed by corporate executives and mountain goats. We know the poles are melting, we know our children are struggling to breathe, we know the black gold is poisoning us, but we can't help ourselves. Being social creatures of the highest order, we create shared realities, linking ideas into theoretical systems, but we allow ourselves to be fooled. Lethal ideas have caused us to commit the most horrific atrocities: slavery, ethnic cleansing, the Holocaust. Periodically, the social norms go awry and only hindsight allows unclouded vision of our behaviour.

Whew, you think. This woman could really use a couple of days of full sun! Perhaps you are right but think about it. The evidence that we are hurting ourselves and killing future generations outright is everywhere. What if we took off the blinders for a minute and faced the reality of our actions? Look around you right now. How many things are turned on that you aren't using? And what about that forkful of food coming at you? Where the heck did it come from? Was the soil poisoned with pesticides now filtering into drinking water to grow it? Did that mouthful kill the songbirds of a valley, the bees, the bacteria, the seeds of plants?

There is nothing the guys like better than a good project, such as pulling a floathouse from the water onto land. Here, a cable is being cut by pounding it against an axe. While this looks dangerous, each man knows how to move and protect himself without putting the next guy at risk.

The children of Echo Bay often make their own toys, and sailing these "stick boats" is a favourite pastime. Building the toys is more than half the fun.

Coastal children take little notice of the cold. Though his legs are brilliant pink from the frigid temperature, Logan Miller is not dissuaded from taking the leap again and again.

A young woman pounds a drift bolt into a log to fasten it in place, as her father tows the float into Echo Bay.

We all have choices. We could each unplug the little power-eaters as we leave home; we can shape the economy by buying from companies that have figured out how *not* to wipe out life. Downsize, eat organic, remember the simple pleasures, be responsible for the impact your money has after it leaves your hand, tear up the lawn and plant kale.

Yes, kale. A beautiful plant of many different types — silver, dark green and even blue — kale will nourish you all year long. Kale requires none of the poisons of your lawn. Add it to soups, fry it in a wok, use it as spinach, make a salad, dry it and pack it with you on expeditions, steam it with rice, wrap it around salmon pâté, snack on a leaf as you hurry down your driveway on your bike and leave it as a legacy when you move. Growing kale is a kiss upon the Earth, not a jab.

Spikes like nails protrude from the bottoms of caulk boots, to allow a person to walk across even the slipperiest of logs. Here a raft of logs is being assembled to create a float.

Our children depend on us to leave an inheritance of living ecosystems, not as a park for them to play in but for their very survival. The Earth and our bodies are all one closely intertwined organism; as fares our planet, so will we fare.

The Web of Life

After living here for 20 years, I see that everything, big or little — whales, ravens, cedar trees, salmon, plankton, huckleberries, maggots, bears, humans — is connected. We are all part of the complex and intricately balanced web of life that has evolved over unknown thousands of years.

A Snapshot in Time

Shafts of sunlight sent parallel lines of essential energy deep into the cold, clear water. Here in the dynamic tideline of Blackfish Sound, the tidal force of the Pacific Ocean slid sensuously along the exhalation of Blackney Passage. Billions of gallons of seawater, forced out of Johnstone Strait, pressed seaward, until the mighty passage would breathe them in again. The roiling choreography of these surface currents sucks deep, seafloor water from its relentless glide across the globe. Numbingly cold, oxygen-depleted but enriched by the rain of a million lives completed on the surface, these ancient waters arch up toward the light to spark life once more.

An eagle fishes close to the forested shoreline.

Through the meeting of living and dead waters, the dark-green back of a 16-kilogram chinook salmon swayed back and forth. This fish was confident in her ability and big enough to intimidate all but the ultimate predator, the orca. This meant she could swim alone, exposed, suspended in the crystalline waters. She was content to circle below the coppery, writhing ball of herring above, oblivious to the gulls, auklets, murres and eagles. At the slightest urge, this salmon would strike deep into the herring and with a mouthful, grow another gram heavier, nurturing the eggs carefully stowed against her spine.

At the next step down the food chain, the herring enacted an alternative strategy. For them there is no desire to reveal a solo silhouette to all below; the only hope here, in the vise of opposing tides, is schoolmates. None could bear to be the outside fish, so each of the thousands nosed furiously inward until those in the middle were forced skyward. Flying, beached upon the solid mass of fish below, these were the offerings to the winged birds. The web-footed birds got the fellows below, and the fish in the middle had no oxygen, all water squeezed out by the mass of imploding mates. A galaxy of scales twinkled down-current, broadcasting the scent of this passage of energy from one layer of life to the next.

Moments later a solid wall emblazoned by a streak of grey arced past the school. This was a warning to all feathered feasters to take wing. Banking left beneath the rising flock, the minke whale parted pleated jaws, rolled to her side and engulfed the school, then expelled the water that had buoyed the fish and slid deep to swallow. The few herring that had escaped darted to lie beneath islands of kelp spinning in the meeting of the waters. Protecting the DNA of a run from deep in Knight Inlet, these fish would carry forth the line. The salmon left the banquet to resume her migration south, pulled by the ripening of her unborn eggs. The auklets struggled to fly home to Pine Island with a payload of herring for growing chicks. The murres found their mothers and paddled obediently behind to await the blossoming of another feast, as the minke rose to exhale a fishy sigh. Thirty seconds had passed in the archipelago.

Gulls lift off as a minke whale engulfs a school of herring and submerges, leaving this upwelling as she closes her jaws.

A school of herring, tightly balled by fish and diving birds. Gull feet can be seen paddling on the surface, as their owners wait for the fish to come within reach of their beaks.

Bull kelp marks all the reefs on this coast. It is a benefit to boaters but more than that, it creates a protected "forest" environment for larval fish, invertebrates and sea otters. There are records of bull kelp "stipes" or stems 36 meters long.

A young male orca "kelping," dragging kelp along his fin and flukes. Probably this feels good to these sensuous animals, scratching the hard-to-reach spots.

This image evokes the sweet scent of spring, when salmonberry flowers attract hummingbirds and the cycle of life renews itself.

A humpback whale breaches. More of them are now coming back into the archipelago every year.

A gray whale melts into the sands of northern Vancouver Island, leaving behind only her enormous structure of bones. Bears gnawed this carcass; crabs, mink, birds and insects also fed on it. Nothing is wasted, nothing simply vanishes.

Dolphins undeniably like to play and treat humans as pool-toys on occasion.

Sooty shearwaters bob quietly at the edge of the Broughton Archipelago in Queen Charlotte Strait, a sure sign that fall is coming.

Herring appear to drop from the sky as an eagle lifts off from a school of herring forced to the surface by diving birds and fish. The eagle will carry these fish back to chicks just beginning to fledge.

Sandhill cranes head south over Eden Island. Their distinctive calls capture my attention once or twice a year if I am lucky, as they follow their age-old route along the eastern edge of the archipelago.

The Pinks

The summer of 2002 was a blissful series of clear, calm days. When I pulled up to the crisp little gillnet boat, Rick and Lynn smiled and waved. "No, we didn't catch any Atlantic salmon last night. Actually, we didn't catch much of anything!" When the fishery closed, they had 12 pink salmon — they should have had a thousand.

A few weeks after the gillnet opening, tour operators taking people into watersheds to watch grizzly bears began asking, "Where are all the pink salmon?" Young cubs were being eaten by starving adults. Tour guests burst into tears, watching as panicked bears searched the river for the calories they required to survive winter. The usual 300 eagles never gathered, and the few that lived in the valleys of Knight Inlet ate seagulls, a poor substitute for the vitamin-endowed flesh of a salmon. "The pinks have crashed" was the phrase of wonder that fall, and in languages as diverse as a bear's growl and an eagle's screech it reverberated through homes, canyons and across open water. But the pink salmon elsewhere came home in glorious abundance. It is time to protect one of the last great wild food resources our planet has bestowed on us.

What is a pink salmon anyway? What's all the fuss? They're just a runt of a salmon, no trophies among them. They fill those tiny cans on the market shelf. Tuna probably taste better anyway, so who cares if the little cans disappear?

Let's take a journey back to the beginning. The tiny bit of life, curled into the shape of a comma, struggles against the rose-tinted membrane that entrapped it. Finally freed, its delicate spinal cord straightens for the first time and begins the gentle sashay that makes this a salmon. Then the little fish becomes restless. Lying in the gravel is no longer enough; she wants to move, craving the taste of something she has never known — salt. In a flood of life she and her brethren emerge under cover of night and pour downriver. Flowing into a cool April sea, the river pushes this tender life out beyond the delta. "Swim and bring home riches from the sea so that I may bear again," is the river's last message as she embeds her scent to guide the fish home.

Spawning pink salmon acclimatize to fresh water after their time in the ocean. They will give up a lifetime of energy when they die, to nourish the coast, and their young will go directly to sea.

A black bear sits beside the Embly River, satiated with pink salmon, full of the calories it needs to survive a winter without eating. During the salmon runs, bears will tolerate each other's presence, crowding around pools to feast.

Twice a year, in June and December, we have extremely high tides. Here, my dogs look wonderingly for the land that always connects us to our ramp.

Sharky breaches near a Steller's sea lion haulout. Though her clan does not eat sea lions, that doesn't mean they don't like to tease them. One sea lion was startled off the rock by Sharky's leap and she darted off, very excited.

Synchronizing their activities is a game and a way of life for Pacific white-sided dolphins. Here, a pair takes a breath in unison while riding the wake of my boat.

The kingfisher blinks in pleased surprise. Appearing suicidal, the blue-and-white bird leaps off her perch and falls headlong into the sea. Gone for an instant, she flutters back to her perch and deftly whacks the silver fish twice, then closes her eyes as it slips down her throat and trips an inner clock: time to make eggs and continue this kingfisher line.

By the first of May dark ribbons of 5-cm fish snake for many kilometres along steep rocky shores and swirl above white-shell seafloors in shallow coves. Young coho, fat and sassy after a year in the stream, position themselves below the baby pinks; brilliant, predatory flashes remove all that are slow, damaged or inferior until only the finest and most robust are left to fan out from the archipelago waters. The sweeps of the growing spotted tails continue to push the unseen masses west. Wherever the pink salmon school, they are continuously honed to perfection by their predators.

Feeding low on the food chain, on plankton blooming under an open ocean sun, these fish avoid the insidious toxins we have unwisely loosed into the atmosphere. They feed as directly upon the sunlight as animal life can, and this they store in their rapidly growing bodies until an internal voice whispers, "Come home to me."

Some forms of life were simply designed to satisfy the masses, and pink salmon are one of these. Returning home, they feed the sea lion pups, nourish the mighty orca, offer a package of protein just the perfect size to be carried into an eagle's nest and sustain communities of humans. If they all made it back into the river, they would not fit, but if none came home at all, this passage of life would become a sweep of death.

Leaping in wriggling abandon, as if swimming up into the clouds, the returning pinks have brought a sense of peace to First Nation elders for 5,000 years; winter survival was assured. Sweeping her massive head, the mother grizzly can smell their arrival on the wind; the cub inside her and the ones wrestling with her now will live to grow. The mink, wolf, raccoon, raven, even the mountain goat and cedar tree will benefit from the nitrogen, phosphorus, fat, protein and

In this unintended double exposure, it is clear that the whale and the river are one organism. Unless the rivers, with their salmon runs, are healthy, we will lose the whales and all the other life forms in between.

minerals surging up the river, timidly at first and then with a rush so great the level of the river itself is raised. As males and females find their perfect match, rosy eggs spill down into the gravel. The water ouzel, a bird that runs along the river bottom, chases these pearls of protein to refuel her motherhood-depleted body.

Insects lay eggs on decomposing ocean protein so that come spring, there will be invertebrates to nourish young coho, chinook, steelhead, trout and sockeye that, unlike the pinks, must stay and feed in the river. Without the pinks there would be no bugs and none of the larger salmon could survive. An eagle takes a bellyful of salmon into the alpine region and leaves some behind to fertilize a clump of grass with nitrogen 15 from the Pacific. And then a hush drifts down the watershed. The eggs are washed clean by oxygen-rich water in gravel beneath ice, snow blankets the forest floor, and it all begins again.

To break this chain of life, to allow wondrous ancient DNA to unravel, to pronounce a death sentence upon innocent life as diverse as snowflakes in a blizzard should be a crime all humanity guards against. Inside that tin beside the tuna is a blueprint for the perpetuity of life — our life, our world, our children's lives.

A fog bank creeps off Queen Charlotte Strait into Cullen Harbour at sunset.

*Silence falls over Cramer Pass
after a mid-winter snowfall.*

A raven patrolling the neighbourhood. The voice of the raven forms an acoustic backdrop to this coast. Their rich languages can be raucous or like the ring of a bell.

Pacific white-sided dolphins and gulls hover over a school of nourishing capelin in Tribune Channel.

The last A-frame in the Broughton Archipelago travels up Cramer Pass toward retirement. This labour-intensive form of logging hired many people, removed only the trees closest to the water and supported small communities. It has been lost to highly mechanized corporate logging, which removes entire forests with very little benefit to local areas.

Fragile Splendour

J wish I could report that all is well in this stunningly beautiful area of the coast, but sadly, the natural balance of life is threatened by some of mankind's activities.

❧

Logging the Salmon Forest

When a river is logged, the first round of impact can come from the loss of living trees. The trees keep water temperatures low with their shading branches, but even more important, their roots absorb and slow the rainfall, preventing floods. After a few years, young trees grow back, shading the water course and sending out new essential roots, but now there are no large trees dying. When a mature tree falls across a river, it creates essential habitat for salmon. A river without logs across it scours all life away, so a second impact is the lack of old, dying trees.

After baby coho salmon hatch, they swim into the tiniest reaches of the rivers, to escape predation by trout and to find

Clear-cut logging in the Viner River watershed devastated the run of chum salmon here.

A logged watershed has lost its crucial function. This stream can't produce salmon, so no salmon can return to feed the forest.

Shawl Bay, just before it was logged, in a December freeze.

food. Frequently, these pools become isolated from the river when water levels are low. The young salmon thrive in these micro-habitats and then swim away when the rains bring the river back to them. But these pools lie on the richest portion of the forest floor, called the "riparian zone." In fact, they are what make these areas so rich; the river valleys grow the most magnificent stands of timber. Without the conifer canopy, the tiny pools in which the coho live become too hot for the fish to survive.

After a forest is removed, a natural succession of plant life occurs, beginning with leafy deciduous species, such as alder and salmonberry bushes. These plants grow quickly, providing essential shade over the streams, bringing water temperatures back down into the salmon's range of survivability. Their roots rebuild the vital lattice that holds the soil on the hills. Without such roots, the rain washes soil into the river where it settles in the gravel and creates a pavement-like surface that cannot hold and incubate salmon eggs. When a salmon tries to dig a "redd" or nest in silted gravel, the eggs don't settle into the nooks and crannies of the gravel; they wash downstream. Elderberry, devil's club and many others of this succession of plant life also feed the bears, elk, mountain goats and deer. The economically coveted young conifers then grow slowly through these pioneering species, feeding on the annual organic decomposition of their deciduous leaves.

However, the forest companies don't want to wait for the natural cycle. They want to start a new conifer forest right away, because the government won't allow a logging company to cut more wood until the replanted seedlings are about 15 feet high. So they try to speed up the cycle. Although they have removed the forest that would otherwise have fed the soil, the companies want to spray pesticides on all the competing species and, without the addition of nutrients, plant the forest they desire — genetically modified conifers. Spraying pesticides near the tiny pools where coho are growing can be lethal to the fish, and coho are struggling against extinction in British Columbia.

An essential piece of coastal equipment — the boomchain — forming here the link between a floathouse and the shore. These chains also corral logs by the millions on their journey from the forests to the mills.

Toxic Chemicals

In 1998 an application was made for a permit to spread solid sewage waste from the city of Vancouver on the floodplains of the Klinaklini River. When I saw the application I thought, "The world is going nuts." Listed in the contents of the sludge were arsenic, copper, heavy metals and lead. The magnificent Klinaklini runs into the head of Knight Inlet and provides spawning habitat not only to salmon, but also to oolichan. The application was eventually withdrawn — too much opposition. But constant vigilance is necessary.

The need to reduce chemicals in our environment became frighteningly evident through research by Graeme Ellis, Lance Barrett-Lennard, Peter Ross and others at the Institute of Ocean Sciences. When Lance took his tissue samples from whales to determine paternity in B.C. orca, I was opposed to his highly intrusive data-collection technique — a dart shot from a crossbow into the side of the whale. The dart took a 200-mg sample of blubber and fell out, floating on the surface for recovery. When I spoke to Lance about "shooting" whales he said, "I'll also use the samples to determine the health of these whales, Alex. We need to know the levels of industrial pollution they're carrying before we can do anything to protect them." To be honest, I didn't believe him. But I was wrong.

In a wake-up call, Lance's samples revealed that the transient orca population were the most contaminated mammal tested on Earth! They were worse than the belugas in the St. Lawrence River, and those whales were considered toxic waste when they died. I was shaken when I learned that the resident fish-eating whales were also highly polluted with PCBs, because I eat exactly what they do and worse, I feed it to my children. Because so much is known about the age and history of each of the 54 whales tested, the research by these men was vastly revealing. They found that while the male whales' level of contamination rose steadily throughout their lives, the females' dropped precipitously when they gave birth. With each baby, the mother transferred a significant portion of her deadly burden to the next generation through gestation and nursing. I was nursing my daughter at the time, so this was a sickening bit of news.

After menopause the toxic load in females begins to build again. The toxin levels found in B.C. whales are high enough to interfere with reproduction, as well as endocrine and immune responses. But where are these chemicals coming from? Some are from pulp mills on the coast, others are from electrical transformers apparently dumped in the sea for disposal and others are drifting in from Asia on currents of air and water. The phrase "spaceship Earth" is real. This planet *is* so small that we are affected by the actions of people everywhere.

The only protection available — to all of us — from these toxins, which climb from species to species up the food chain, is to eat low on the pyramid of life. The healthiest salmon, therefore, is the short-lived pink salmon, which not only grows fast, minimizing the bio-accumulation of contaminants, but also feeds low on the food chain itself. We can no longer treat our surroundings as being separate from us, because the environment deep within our bodies is undergoing the same degradations as the environment outside us.

Salmon Farming

When salmon farming first appeared in the Broughton Archipelago, it seemed a good idea. Echo Bay was promised jobs, new families to help keep the one-room school open and relief from fishing pressure on wild fish. The community was advised that it could decide where farms would not be allowed. The future looked rosy. But instead, the salmon farms were placed in zones where the wild salmon schooled, prawns were most abundant, whales spent the summers and rock cod lived. The archipelago was damaged.

Salmon farms differ fundamentally from land-based farms; their effluent flows directly, untreated, into contact with wild species. Epidemics in wild fish are extremely rare, because when pathogens strike, the sick drop out of the school and are eaten by predators. Intensive farming, however, breaks natural laws of density and survival of the fittest. Salmon are designed to move. Small bays, which might support a few hundred salmon in intermittent bursts throughout the year, are now filled with up to 1 million stationary salmon. This is the best thing to happen to fish pathogens on this coast since the glaciers receded. The feces of the crowded fish pass over each other's gills. Because the fish are confined and unable to migrate, pathogens accumulate into a rich broth. Disease is nature's relentless response to overcrowding, so the farmers have to resort to drugs. Antibiotics can keep most farm salmon alive long enough to reach restaurant size, but they leave the fish contagious, and they can spread diseases into marine currents used by the wild salmon.

Wherever there are salmon farms, there have been epidemic outbreaks of the salmon-specific sea louse *Lepeophtheirus salmonis*. Entire runs of salmonids (Atlantic salmon and sea trout) have been affected by sea lice proliferation near salmon farms in Ireland, Scotland and Norway. Sea lice have been historically considered harmless to wild fish: wild Pacific salmon become infected with them in the open ocean and when they return to spawn, the lice die as the salmon enters fresh water. But salmon farms have dramatically altered sea lice ecology.

As the adult, river-bound wild salmon pass fish farms in the fall, their lice shed larvae, some of which attach to the farm salmon. Over the winter months these lice reproduce exponentially, finding hosts easily in the unnaturally crowded net pens. By spring the farm salmon are hosting lice that shed

An invader – an Atlantic salmon in Scott Cove Creek. Hundreds of thousands of Atlantics have escaped from salmon farms to survive and breed along the coast, disrupting the fine balance of the five Pacific salmon species and the rivers they have co-created.

Salmon farm nets are washed in the big, slow-turning drum and the effluent is poured overboard into Fife Sound through which the wild salmon migrate to their rivers. Any diseases present can easily pass into the spawning and nursery grounds of the wild stocks.

Totes full of "morts" (dead farm salmon) ooze rotting liquid, attracting flies which could spread any viruses or bacteria far afield.

Industrial feedlots require chemicals to limit the explosive growth of bacteria, parasites and viruses. The difference with salmon farming is that the feedlot flows directly into the ocean and into contact with wild fish, birds and marine mammals. This barrel of formic acid sits on a mort float; the dead fish are brought here to be doused in the acid to try to stop diseases from spreading.

billions of lice larvae, just as the tender young wild salmon pass through the farm nets on their way out to sea.

This scenario has played out worldwide, wherever salmon farms are placed in wild salmon waters. Norwegian scientists say they expected this to happen to us. But salmon farms do not need the lice that proliferate on their fish, and they do not need to destroy the wild salmon. All that is required here is separation between the farms and the very small wild salmon.

Farming fish has been practised for thousands of years but not in the manner now under way on many temperate coasts worldwide. Traditionally, fish that eat vegetable matter were raised, such as carp or tilapia. Chinese fish farms have cycled waste from vegetable crops through their fish and then used the waste from the fish to fertilize the next vegetable crop. This sustainable, closed-loop system created protein. However, salmon are carnivores and it takes two to five pounds of wild fish to produce one pound of farm salmon. This represents a net loss of global protein because most of the fish used to make feed pellets are high-quality food, fit for human consumption.

Farm salmon flesh is dyed pink; it is high in PCBs and low in omega oils so its food value is questionable, but there are additional considerations for human health. Many of the net pens in the Broughton Archipelago have been painted with Flexgard XI, whose active ingredient is 26.5% cuprous oxide, to prevent growth of seaweeds, barnacles and mussels. The label for this paint sports a skull and crossbones and this warning: "Toxic to aquatic organisms. Do not contaminate water. Do not allow chips or dust generated during paint removal to enter water." However, it is painted onto the nets submerged in water and has to be reapplied periodically because it all flakes off. As the densely crowded farm salmon gulp their feed pellets, they can also ingest this toxic paint drifting from all sides of the pen.

Ivermectin has been used by salmon farmers to rid their crowded stocks of sea lice. Four nanograms of ivermectin per litre of water kills shrimp (that's one ounce per 10,000 Olympic-sized swimming pools) and though B.C. salmon farmers are prohibited from putting ivermectin directly into the water as a "pesticide," they are allowed to soak it into food pellets as a "pharmaceutical." On February 7, 2000, 7,000 farm salmon died from an overdose of ivermectin in a pen in Wells Passage, illustrating the narrow margin between efficacy and toxicity for this drug.

Three escaped Atlantics caught in Scott Cove Creek had red-rimmed, pus-encrusted sores. An independent lab reported that the cause was the bacteria *Serratia*. This bacteria, common in human sewage, was found in farm salmon in Scotland when the crew sewers leaked. A provincial report released in April 2000 on compliance in B.C.'s salmon farms found that 75% of salmon farms were not disposing of their human sewage at a safe distance from the farms. I received an anonymous call (one of many from people inside the industry and government) saying when they flushed dye down their toilets, it came up inside the net pens.

Salmon farming does not need to be destructive; it is the net-pen system that creates problems. There are communities on this coast that would welcome land-based salmon farms. There the farms could continue to offer employment benefits while allowing wild salmon and the myriad life-forms they support to thrive.

An Empty River

In late summer I stood on a bridge overlooking a stretch of spawning gravel as wide as the Island Highway. The light was perfect so I could see clearly into the river, shallow for lack of water. I saw two trout and four coho seeking cover under the bridge, but the stones of the Wahpeeto River, tributary to the Wakeman River, bore no sign of salmon. Each smooth stone wore a blanket of algae, like a dusting of new-fallen green snow. These pebbles had not felt the caress of female salmon digging redds to lay their eggs. Pink salmon are known for their prodigious ability to move rocks. They are small but so abundant, they are major architects in the rivers where they spawn.

One set of grizzly tracks went one way along the bank. The bear had not turned, had not entered the river, had not found any food here. There was one lower fish jaw on the beach, but no scent, no eagles, no seagulls. Only one lone water ouzel slipped beneath the water searching for eggs. It is hard to prove the absence of something in science, but the scene below me spoke more eloquently than I ever could. No pulse was beating here. No nutrients were coming upstream here, only running down. The insects required to feed the coho and chinook, which need a year in the rivers before going to sea, were not hatching; no insect eggs were being laid in rich salmon flesh. Another 12 months would pass before food could come upstream again. Lean times were upon the Wakeman Valley. Pink salmon were down again drastically for the second consecutive year; the remaining stocks could not replenish themselves nor their rivers.

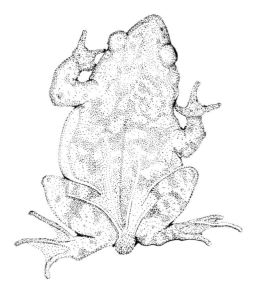

Young pink salmon are badly infested with sea lice only near salmon farms. Their populations are crashing in heavily farmed waters.

Extinction

On June 5, 2001, a fishing-lodge owner and keen observer of fish, Chris Bennett, brought me two tiny salmon, a pink and a chum. One had 16 sea lice sucking its life juices away, the other 19. They looked like pincushions. I started sampling and as I looked at each tiny fish under a magnifying glass, my heart broke. The average load of lice was 10.77 per fish, with some covered in 65.

Since then I have been studying an unprecedented appearance of sea lice on wild juvenile salmon in the heavily salmon-farmed waters of the Broughton Archipelago. After identifying the epidemic in 2001, a cohort of authors and I looked at pink and chum fry coastwide and found sea lice only on young salmon near salmon farms. In 2003, 11 salmon farms were left fallow in the Broughton and sea lice numbers fell dramatically and significantly. In 2004 the farm salmon are back in the pens, and the lice are back with a vengeance. The relationship is undeniable. The Department of Fisheries and Oceans did a study when the farms were empty and reported that juvenile salmon with lice were more robust than those without lice. The scientific community at large finds this ridiculous.

Tribune Channel is a long, narrow waterway dotted by five salmon farms. Millions of tiny pink salmon entered the east end of Tribune in the spring of 2004, but almost none swam out the west end. Every morning I picked up the dying from a short stretch of Tribune. Listless, emaciated, so stunned they did not hear my boat or see my hand reaching for them, these fish would never go to sea. As a young graduate student here told me every evening, "It's carnage out there."

I know there is a great temptation to disregard my work and warnings, but I am certain I am measuring the local extinction of the odd-year cycle of Area 12 Mainland pink salmon. I have been absolutely correct for two years now on the size of this stock's collapse. The reason I have been right is not because I am a great scientist, but because the damage is so huge that anyone can see it.

The number of infected fish accurately predicts how many pink salmon will not return to spawn. The fall of 2004 will see a good pink salmon return to the Broughton Archipelago because these are the fish that went to sea when the salmon farms were fallow. But if their offspring have to swim out through a sea of sea lice, a 5 million-strong population of pink salmon will cease to exist.

This extinction threatens the bloodstream of this ecosystem, the nutrient-delivery mechanism, the food of countless species: the pink salmon. As the cycle of pink salmon incubates within the gravel this winter, we can contemplate whether we truly *never* want to see this run again. That the Broughton pinks are dying out during a regime of extreme abundance on the rest of the coast is a warning so blinding, so bright, only those determined to ignore it could possibly look away and allow it to happen.

The Corporation and the Individual

When I look at a corporation I see an animal. They are beasts of our own making that violate every natural law because, while they exist exclusively in the two dimensions of a piece of paper, they feed in the three dimensions of the living world. When the corporate beast's appetite is finished with an ecosystem that has been drained of its essential elements, the corporation is untouched by the death throes of the life it fed upon. It simply lifts its head momentarily, before descending into another energy-rich natural habitat. There is no possible way this can work. In the not-too-distant future all the natural systems we depend on will stop supporting life.

Do we really have to fell the forests, pollute the sea with biohazards, drill out the oil at the risk of all life? Couldn't we simply find a way to thrive as life around us has? I think we can. We are part of life on Earth, not at odds with it. Our true wealth lies around us, growing as no investment we could ever bank. Perhaps we need to pause and think — how wealthy will we be if we lose all this?

As the corporate footprint sinks deeper into the Broughton Archipelago, I have felt panic, but one should never underestimate the power of love. I feel gratitude that my home is inhabited by people who love this place and have shown willingness to take a stand to protect her.

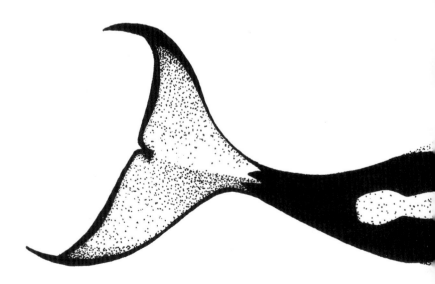

Salmon womb – a wild river in a wild place. The Franklin River at the head of Knight Inlet hosts gatherings of eagles, bears, salmon, oolichan and many other species. Places like this nourish British Columbia in ways people in cities and towns have forgotten. Europeans would love to have such wellsprings of life!

Hope for the Future

Now that we understand the negative effects of some of our actions, many people are working to save the coast. With our love and attention, it may yet be returned to its natural richness and beauty.

❧

Whales Again!

On a December afternoon in 1999 a sweet, singsong note came over the underwater speaker in my house. Adrenaline chased by disbelief raced through my nervous system. It must have been one of the inflated bumpers squeaking between the boat and the dock, I thought. Then it came again. "Oh my god! That's a whale for sure." I bundled Clio, grabbed a coat and rushed out the door, falling full-length on the wet wood of my dock. Collecting my feet beneath me, I made it to the boat. By looking, stopping to listen underwater and then moving again, I found a whale. The light was very dim this near to the solstice, and it was so cold that my binoculars fogged every time I lifted them

A fat and happy young orca appears to float on the water's surface. Whales are willing to tolerate much of our damaging ways, from pollution to loud boats, but they do require food. If we want to keep them as neighbours, we have to make sure they too can make a living in the waters we share.

to the warmth of my eyes. I couldn't see the fins that were approaching me well enough to identify them, so I lowered the hydrophone and just recorded.

The spray flew off their fins as they sped past my boat. This was the first time in five years that I had heard the voices of A clan in the archipelago. Tears of joy blended with the drops of rain pelting against my face. The salmon farmers' underwater acoustic harassment devices had been turned off for over a year. It had taken the A-clan whales a year to take a look at the archipelago again. I was jubilant. I wished them well and hoped they would find these waters habitable and maybe come through again soon.

A few nights later I woke from a deep sleep to the haunting calls of whales again. Then over the next three weeks the whales went by my house once every few days. My reason for being here became clear again.

Helping the Salmon

The Viner River once called home more than 70,000 chum salmon, and now only hundreds come her way. But this is up from tens so we are hopeful. There is no substitute for a truly wild run, but in the face of all we have done to the salmon, taking a small proportion of fish out of a run and boosting survival rates in a hatchery may give the fish the precious time that will make the difference. Hatcheries are rightfully coming under increasing scrutiny, because once a human decides which fish eggs and sperm combine, the fish

population drifts away from its wild perfection. However, in some cases we hope that protecting DNA from the very high mortality that salmon suffer during their life as eggs and freshly hatched alevins can maintain a fish population while its river stabilizes.

On a fall day we went on an expedition up the Viner to collect salmon eggs. The ravens were talking. Cackles, bells, screams and growls came from the treetops. They have a language that is theirs alone, though the rest of the forest listens to them closely. They are the sentinels, and many furry ears no doubt understood the sounds coming from the treetops: "Humans

Pink salmon fan out in the Ahta River, each seeking the perfect place to dig a "redd" or nest, and deposit their precious eggs. As the eggs leave their mothers' bodies, the next generation begins to feed its world, because some eggs will roll downstream to feed trout, birds and insects.

An orca naps on a glorious summer day in Tribune Channel.

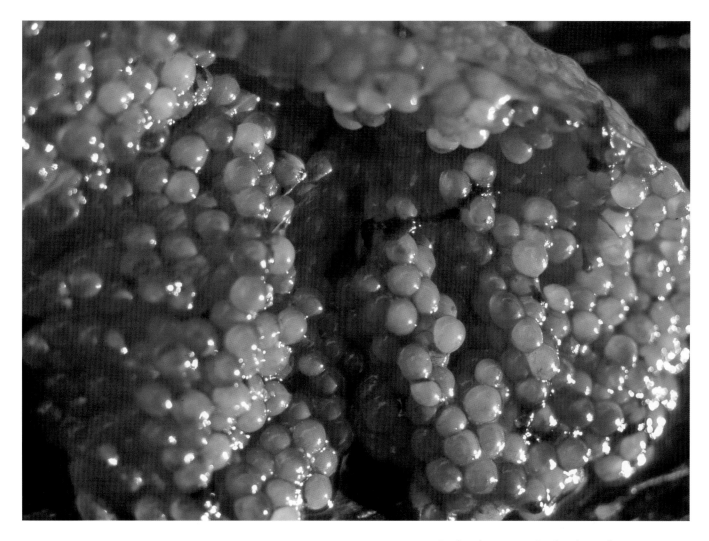

Pink salmon roe. Pink salmon have 1,500 eggs per female; they are an essential artery of energy.

are here on the banks of our banquet." The Viner River cuts deep into the western shore of Gilford Island, originating in a mere crease on the west face of Mount Reid. It is a gentle river, wide-hipped and alder-shaded, the perfect place for chum salmon to spawn. Chums are large, with slender tails, not nearly as athletic as the coho or chinook. We could see their silver, tiger-striped forms streaming upriver, resting beneath sweeps of cedar and fir hanging over the bank, digging redds and chasing each other.

Glen Neidrauer dragged the beach seine net onto a small gravel bar and Claudia Maas, who runs the coho- and chum-enhancement hatchery in Scott Cove, waded to her armpits, careful not to lose her footing in the relentless seaward flow. The bright white corks that float the net snaked out into the

Tiny coho fry from the Scott Cove hatchery are released from a bucket into a wild creek.

dark-brown water. As the net came ashore the water we had corralled began to swirl, then froth, then come alive as 15 chum salmon came to us. They slithered up the beach, over the net and against our legs.

Most of the fish in the net had already spawned so we only counted them, checked their condition and then released them. A stunning, deeply reddened coho was released and one lone male pink salmon. He had a lovely hump and would be considered ever so handsome by a female, if only there was one to catch his eye. His hump would proclaim his successful life: "I went to sea and returned with this much extra"; it would demonstrate that his genes were the best. The male chum salmon knew how to use their teeth, and one turned and bit me. I deserved it and though it hurt and blood ran down my arm, I felt connected for an instant to a fish that held my greatest respect.

Just before Christmas, Claudia, Billy Proctor and I, with children in tow, did our best to dig salmon redds and pour dawn-tinted chum salmon eggs into the gravel. I love doing that. I know it's my species that has hurt their river and I know digging redds with a shovel and not a tail is unnatural, but I can't escape the sense of hope each of those tiny eggs holds. The Viner has become silted with the run-off of unstable, heavily logged slopes, and much of her spawning beds can no longer hold and caress tiny eggs. We cannot give them back the lost diversity of this run, but we can give them the chance to rebuild, by taking their eggs and planting them in the river above the worst of the damage.

In the spring we returned to the Viner to count the surviving young salmon. Billy slung the little seine net over his shoulder and scampered down the bank. There was no debate among this team. Billy said, "Here," and we stopped. Claudia and Billy expertly threaded out the net and slowly swept it across an empty pool. Chum fry and yearling coho smolts materialized in the cold water. Gently the net was slipped away and the little fellows were left to the challenges of their life.

Stewardship

In Echo Bay we have formed a stream stewardship group. We check the streams, measure their attributes, watch for salmon obstructions and fix any impacts we can. I would like to suggest this is something everyone near a stream should try. Eric Nelson, a log salvager, could tell any species of wood from half a mile away, but now he can read a river's health by the composition of its bugs. If it's got predator species, it's a healthy system. If the pH is right, fish will thrive; if not, something needs to be done. Our school is now involved in monitoring the stream behind the playground. The Department of Fisheries and Oceans can

Two residents of Echo Bay dig redds under the watchful eye of hatchery manager Claudia Maas. While many people squander the riches bestowed upon us by the wild salmon, far more are willing to do what it takes to give these fish a chance.

Volunteer Chris Bennett stands in a fall freshet, trying to catch coho broodstock in an effort to re-establish a run of wild coho. It was wiped out when a logger simply left a dam in the river after he was finished his work.

At first light a seiner leaves the Broughton, heading for the packing plant in Port Hardy. It is transporting the richness of the ocean to people who live far from saltwater.

get you started. This is one of their best initiatives. There are too many streams for the government to care for, repair, watch over and assist, but there are many of us spread along the coast and this is a job that can bring great joy. Form your own group or go it alone, but if possible take stewardship of a trickle near you.

An Invitation

For the miracle of change for the better to occur, the fuel source must be love. Not wealth, not fame, not job security, not hate. And there is one other ingredient essential to success — something worth fighting for. Certainly the wild salmon are that. They are a gift to all life on Earth. They bring

Young Siwiti rises boisterously to the surface as her family travels up Knight Inlet. Young orca have a pinkish cast to their white spots, which gradually fades to white as their insulating blubber layer thickens.

prosperity wherever they swim, a food source not meted out by corporate hands. They are ours, and we work for them.

Some who make their living in the Broughton Archipelago think we should not talk about our problems because this might hurt tourism. I can understand their point. But the Broughton is no less beautiful in her hour of need. She lies before me now, in shades of swirling grey, deep forest greens and silver seas. Her white clam beaches are just as inviting, loons still call and wolves still howl. But without the currency of visitors' movements into the Broughton, I think she will be traded away to an industry designed toward instability: able to endure boom and bust but capable of leaving fatal tracks.

So I invite everyone to come here, especially in kayaks and sailboats. Fall in love and breathe life into this area. Come to the Broughton as never before; help to strengthen tourism and tourism operators; put the Broughton on the map as *the* place to see. Maybe you will carry life into these waters as the salmon should be doing. Maybe each one of us has become essential to this place.

Hope

Some time ago I was given the opportunity to meet Jane Goodall. I was spellbound by my childhood idol. She radiated grace, and the wisdom of the Earth. When a lull in the conversation opened, I stepped forward and asked, "Jane, do you think there is hope?" Her answer came back crystal clear, "Yes."

As I look at my children, a son in university and a daughter who still falls asleep in my arms, I find myself thinking indeed, there must be hope for our species. My study of whales has led me to the understanding that we now stand, as a species, at a crossroads. Can we see our own coming extinction and avert it, or will we follow the more traditional path and leap blindly over the edge? I can only say I am thrilled to be alive at this moment in history, because millennia pass between such decisive moments on Earth. The power of one is all we have — but we all have it.